HEAVEN ON THE HALF SHELL

THE STORY OF THE NORTHWEST'S LOVE AFFAIR WITH THE OYSTER

DAVID G. GORDON, NANCY E. BLANTON, AND TERRY Y. NOSHO

WASHINGTON SEA GRANT PROGRAM

AND WESTWINDS PRESS®

Library of Congress Cataloging-in-Publication Data

Gordon, David G. (David George), 1950–
   Heaven on the half shell : the story of the Northwest's love affair with the
oyster / by David G. Gordon, Nancy E. Blanton, and Terry Y. Nosho.
      p. cm.
   ISBN 1-55868-550-2
   1. Oyster industry—Northwest, Pacific. I. Blanton, Nancy E.
II. Nosho, Terry Y. III. Title.

HD9472.O83 U525 2001
338.3'7244'09795—dc21   2001035030

Co-published by
Washington Sea Grant Program
Office of Marine Environmental and
   Resource Programs
College of Ocean and Fishery Sciences
University of Washington
3716 Brooklyn Avenue N.E.
Seattle, Washington 98105-6716
206-543-6600
seagrant@u.washington.edu

WestWinds Press®
An imprint of Graphic Arts Center
   Publishing Company
P.O. Box 10306
Portland, Oregon 97296-0306
503-226-2402
www.gacpc.com

Design: Robyn Ricks, Washington Sea Grant Program

Printed in Hong Kong

Front cover: (clockwise from left): *Oyster shuckers in the 1800s; A prime example
of a Pacific oyster; Modern-day harvesters at low tide; A platter of Puget Sound
oysters on the half shell.* Title page: *Working Willapa Bay's oyster beds during a
nighttime low tide.* Page 2: *Emptied oyster shells cover a Pacific Northwest beach.*
Page 3: *Skiffs filled with farm-raised oysters, circa 1930.* Page 159: *A man and his
mollusks.* Back cover: *A Pacific oyster au naturel.*

CONTENTS

FOREWORD *by Kenneth K. Chew*

Kenneth K. Chew, Associate
Dean, College of Ocean and
Fishery Sciences, University
of Washington, and Director,
Western Regional Aquaculture
Center, Seattle

I never thought that a book of this nature would be considered in my lifetime. But here it is—a colorful and informative account covering 150 years of oystering along the west coast of North America. And it's long overdue.

Being involved with oyster research and education at the University of Washington for over 38 years has made me keenly aware of the shellfish industry and its part in the identity of Pacific Northwest industries and economies. I have worked and interacted with many pioneering oyster researchers and growers over the years, and certainly they have left a lasting legacy for their hard work, persistence, and battles to keep the industry alive.

This rich and thought-provoking book tells of the labors of these pioneers and the rewards we all therefore share today. It reflects the demands of the various species that have entered the scene over the past century and discusses nutritional values, taste, ways to gauge the quality of environment and water, and overall impact of oysters on economics, locally, regionally, and nationally.

This book is not a scientific treatise, nor does it attempt to be one. Rather, the text and archival photographs offer an engaging portrayal of the significant events that have shaped the oyster industry in northern California, Oregon, Washington, British Columbia, and Alaska. This story is articulated capably by the authors, with intriguing input from archived literature and from old-timers who are still around and have reviewed the book for authenticity.

One need only browse through *Heaven on the Half Shell* to appreciate the magnitude and sweep of this time-honored endeavor, oystering. I'm confident that the book will satisfy a wide range of readers—not just oyster growers but anyone interested in learning more about what goes on in the Northwest at the water's edge.

I applaud Washington Sea Grant Program for taking on the challenge of putting together this book. And to you, the reader, I say, "Eat oysters and enjoy this book!"

PREFACE

The story of this book starts with scrapbooks. Four leather-bound volumes of newspaper clippings and other print tidbits had been assembled by Earl Brenner of Olympia, Washington, during his 60-year career as an oyster grower.

Earl R. Brenner
(1921–2000)

We learned of these scrapbooks from Earl's son Bruce, the current president of the J. J. Brenner Oyster Company, the oldest continuously operating oyster enterprise on Washington's Puget Sound. Bruce telephoned us one day, asking if we were interested in looking at the volumes. Earl was approaching the end of his long life, Bruce explained, and he wanted his personal record of his years in the oyster industry to be passed to appreciative hands.

We were deeply moved by Earl's generosity, his wheelchair-bound condition, and his passion to preserve what he'd begun in the 1930s and continued into the early 1960s: an informal history of the oyster industry in the Pacific Northwest. We gratefully accepted the scrapbooks, agreeing to make several full-sized copies—one for exhibit, another for the Brenners, and a third for the University of Washington. The original scrapbooks would be sent to the University's historical archives for safe-keeping.

As we studied the Brenner scrapbooks, we became painfully aware of how much of the oyster industry's record of achievements had already been lost, largely due to neglect. Many of the industry's most distinguished historians, the sons and daughters of the pioneering oyster farmers, had passed away in recent years. Along with them went the remembrances—the tales of their lives on the oyster beds, the stories about the first shipments of seed oysters from Japan, the anecdotes about the war years, when Willapa Bay's residents worked around the clock preparing protein-rich shellfish to feed our troops at home and overseas.

The next week, in the Seattle offices of Washington Sea Grant Program, we vowed to do everything we could to record that history. We made appointments to interview some of the elder oystermen and began soliciting donations of old photographs, can labels, restaurant menus—anything that could give an insight into the early history of oysterdom. We also hosted a luncheon for the region's senior oyster growers at a restaurant in Shelton, one of several historic oyster-growing communities. Among our guests were several third-, fourth-, and fifth-generation oystermen, many still working the shoreline plots deeded to their ancestors in the mid-1800s. Also in attendence were others with less extensive but equally interesting careers in oyster farming, such as the restaurant's owner, Xinh Dwelley (who, before opening her restaurant, had won the West Coast's oyster shucking competition two years in a row), and ourselves.

The results of our inquiry into the time-honored traditions of oyster farming are presented in this book. Like Earl Brenner's collection of clippings, our volume contains a rich bouillabaisse of regional history, local lore, scientific data, and first-person reports. Unlike Earl's book, this one draws on much earlier sources, reaching back in time to an era predating the first European immigrants to the Northwest. In this respect, the book is unique. While others have assembled personal histories of their geographic regions, to our knowledge this is the only detailed exploration of the oyster industry throughout the four states and the adjacent Canadian province that make up the coastal Northwest. Amassing material for this broad overview has been a mammoth task. Even after countless hours of library research, numerous interviews by phone and in person, and many visits to the oyster beds themselves, we've still barely dipped beneath the surface of what has proved to be an ocean of information about the oyster and the people who cultivate it.

Of course, the history of the Northwest oyster industry does not end with this book. It continues to be written as oyster growers and their shellfish stocks adapt to changing environmental and economic conditions. If there are central themes to this book, they are human ingenuity and endurance—of the oyster grower's ability to overcome obstacles, both natural and human-caused, to sustainably and profitably harvest the bounty of Northwest shores. Whether battling the devastating effects of shellfish disease, the impacts of overharvesting, or the uncertainty of local, national, and world markets, the oyster grower has emerged victorious, earning a respectable title for himself or herself: a farmer of the intertidal. It is to every one of these tireless workers, living or dead, that we respectfully dedicate this book.

In Remembrance of William Henry Pierre Sr.

Washington Sea Grant Program is grateful for the generosity of the Pierre Family, without whom this book project could not have been realized.

Born on March 5, 1912, in Aberdeen, Washington, William Henry Pierre Sr. first supported himself by digging razor clams for canneries in the coastal community of Copalis Beach, Washington. He later attended the University of Washington's School of Business, then served as general manager for New York Life Insurance in Boise, Idaho, and Spokane, Washington.

In 1946, three former fraternity brothers encouraged William Sr. to open a Ford franchise in Seattle. He took their advice and the following year opened Bill Pierre Ford in Lake City, Washington. The business grew exponentially. Until his death in 1997, William Sr. remained active in the automobile business, periodically taking time off to pursue his passions— fishing, hunting, and, of course, razor-clamming at Copalis Beach. Bill Pierre Ford is now owned and operated by his two sons, Jamie and William Jr.

William Henry Pierre Sr.

(1912–1997)

Major Oyster Growing Areas in the Pacific Northwest

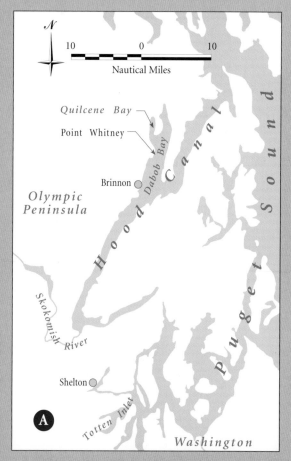

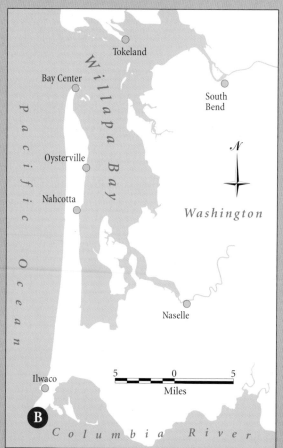

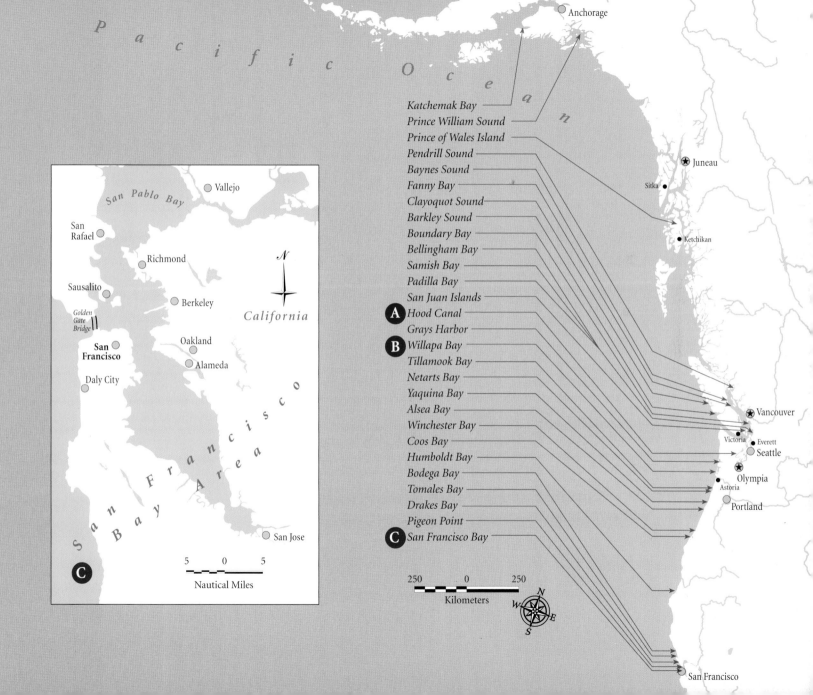

Pacific Ocean

Katchemak Bay
Prince William Sound
Prince of Wales Island
Pendrill Sound
Baynes Sound
Fanny Bay
Clayoquot Sound
Barkley Sound
Boundary Bay
Bellingham Bay
Samish Bay
Padilla Bay
San Juan Islands
A Hood Canal
Grays Harbor
B Willapa Bay
Tillamook Bay
Netarts Bay
Yaquina Bay
Alsea Bay
Winchester Bay
Coos Bay
Humboldt Bay
Bodega Bay
Tomales Bay
Drakes Bay
Pigeon Point
C San Francisco Bay

Anchorage

Juneau

Sitka

Ketchikan

Vancouver

Victoria
Everett
Seattle

Olympia
Astoria
Portland

San Francisco

250   0   250
Kilometers

San Pablo Bay

Vallejo

San Rafael

Richmond

Sausalito

Berkeley

N

Golden Gate Bridge

California

Oakland

San Francisco

Alameda

Daly City

San Francisco Bay Area

San Jose

5   0   5
Nautical Miles

C

Oysterville Sea Farms

Willapa Bay
SMOKED OYSTERS

WELCOME!

OPEN
Please Come In!

I. An Oysterman's Lot

Why, then the world's mine oyster,
Which I with sword will open.

—*William Shakespeare,* The Merry Wives of Windsor

Consider the oyster grower, as author and epicure M. F. K. Fisher might've said—a person who spends the best years of his or her life in the service of a cold-blooded animal with a calcium shell.

Clad in rubber rain gear and thick-soled boots, oyster growers spend hours on blustery beaches, constructing beds in which young oysters will slumber and the grown-ups will reproduce. They stand watch, night and day, to protect the occupants of those beds from predators. They do everything possible to protect the oysters from pollution, disease, and the occasional oyster pirate—the midnight marauder who helps himself to shellfish in someone else's beds.

If all goes as planned, an oysterman's beds will thrive, and the oysters in them will grow plump and ripe. In a few years, the oysters will reward the hard-working grower with their meat.

Businesses (opposite) and placards (below) in the community of Oysterville advertise the oysterman's delectable contributions.

WHEN IN HONOLULU BUY PINEAPPLES

WHEN IN OYSTERVILLE BUY OYSTERS

British Columbia's hard-working aquaculturists (opposite) harvest an estimated $11 million worth of oysters each year. Shellfish culture is the top employer on Cortes Island and one of the largest employers in the Baynes Sound area.

It's an oysterman's prerogative to keep the shellfish he's raised or to sell them to another party—perhaps a neighbor, a passer-by, a seafood retailer, or a wholesale broker—for a reasonable sum. The monetary gains from these transactions are usually modest. But a few fortunes have been made on such dealings. A few more have been lost … and won again. That's the nature of the oyster business.

Making money is just one reason folks in the Pacific Northwest farm oysters. "The business is an excellent one, but the oysterman who makes a good thing of it fully earns every cent that he gets," says Eldon Griffin, in the 1941 publication, *Oysters Have Eyes.*

What, then, draws oyster farmers to the water's edge at dawn or in the dead of night? What makes them work so hard, often in miserable weather, to keep their oysters fat and fit? What makes the rest of us clamor for that small tidbit of flesh, cradled by the smooth inner nacre of an oyster's thickly sculpted shell? One answer's obvious: the ambrosial taste of the Northwest oyster, a flavor unsurpassed by any other of the world's edible shellfish. Equally compelling are the health benefits from

adding oysters to our diets. Raw or cooked, oysters are low in calories, high in vitamins and minerals, and easier to digest than red meat. The high iron, copper, and zinc content of oysters makes these morsels instrumental in the prevention and treatment of anemia, and, because of their iodine content, they've been credited with preventing goiter. Oysters are superb sources of calcium, phosphorus, potassium, and vitamin A, the antioxidant believed to help prevent cancer and guard against bacterial infections. They are rich in omega-3 fatty acids, believed instrumental in the development and function of the brain, retina of the eye, and sperm. Even their shells are considered therapeutic. Oyster shell is used in traditional Chinese medicine to relieve hypertension, heart palpitations, insomnia, dizziness, blurred vision, cold sweats, and swollen lymph glands.

Need another reason to dine on oysters? "They add years to your life," according to M. F. K. Fisher, who, in her book *Consider the Oyster*, also cites the healthful shellfish's longstanding reputation as an aphrodisiac. The alleged role of the oyster in fueling the fires of love may be related to the high zinc content of oyster meat.

Or it may be based solely on the oyster's association with the ancient Greek love goddess Aphrodite, said to have been born from the sea. Regardless of the reasoning, M. F. K. Fisher writes, "there is an astounding number of men, and some of them have graduated from Yale and even Princeton, who know positively that oysters are an aphrodisiac … one of the best. They can tell of countless chaps whose powers have been increased nigh unto the billy goat's, simply from eating raw, cold oysters." Fact or fiction? We'll leave it to you to decide.

WHAT'S AN OYSTER?

An oyster is a mollusk—a shelled invertebrate (or animal without a backbone) in the same zoological phylum, Mollusca, as the mussel, clam, abalone, snail, octopus, and squid. Oysters are also classified as bivalves, which means that their shells are in two parts, or "valves," held together by an elastic ligament hinge. In comparison, a snail wears a one-piece shell, placing it in

Densely packed oyster flats (opposite) create unique intertidal habitats, occupied by an assortment of fish and invertebrates. The young of another favorite Northwest shellfish, the Dungeness crab, frequently settle among the oysters' crags and hide from predators while they grow.

the class Gastropoda. An oyster makes its own shell, secreting calcium and other materials from glandular tissue in the shellfish's soft flesh.

Shellfish biologists have identified about 500 species of bivalves from the waters of the West Coast. Only six of these species are oysters, and only one—the Olympia oyster—is native to our shores. The others were brought to the Pacific Northwest by oyster growers within the past 150 years. But that's another story—one that happens to be the focus of this book.

Wholly adapted for an aquatic existence, oysters have gills for breathing. As water is drawn across the gills, these feathery organs also collect particles of food from the water that surrounds them. Some species live in deep enough water to avoid being exposed to the air at low tide. Those that settle in shallower seas must deal periodically with exposure to the elements. They clamp their two-part shells tightly together, using their powerful adductor muscle to hold tight (the dark spots on the inside of an empty shell are the points where the ends of this muscle once adhered). Now sealed, the oyster can retain enough moisture to stay high and dry

for hours, or if necessary, several days. The shell's thick calcium carbonate covering will also save the oyster from the beaks of seagulls and shorebirds.

Oysters can snap their shells closed with lightning speed and the power of a vise. To open a live oyster, a knife blade must be inserted between the shells and the adductor muscle severed. This process of opening an oyster and removing the meat is called "shucking"—a word that invites all sorts of capricious wordplay.

By some standards, an oyster leads a dream life. It doesn't have to hunt for food, but simply waits for the tide to bring the next serving. Breakfast in bed never ends. Snug in a subtidal channel or secure on a soggy mudflat, an oyster can feed at its leisure, filtering up to eight gallons of food-rich salt water per hour. That food, by the way, is called phytoplankton—tiny aquatic plants and animals that live in the sea.

While there's not excitement in an oyster's life, it seems to keep the little mollusk healthy and happy as a…clam. Some of the longest-lived animals on our planet are bivalves, with record-holders such as the geoduck and giant tridacna clam capable of attaining

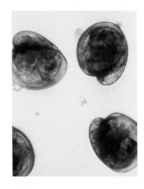

Here's where the oyster industry begins: with oyster larvae prior to settling down.

160 and 200 years respectively. Unless something unexpected happens, an oyster can live about 50 years—real proof that life in the slow lane has rewards.

Most oysters are hermaphroditic—that is, they have both male and female reproductive organs. In some species, they first mature into males (in about one year), and then change to females after spawning. Alternation of sexes apparently continues throughout life. Male eastern oysters release sperm into the water, but the eggs are fertilized within the branchial chamber, a space between the gills of the female. The brood—an average of 250,000 to 300,000 larvae—continues to develop for about 10 days before the female eastern oyster discharges them with convulsive gasps into the world outside her shell. Olympia and Pacific oysters employ a slightly different strategy called "broadcast spawning." For these species, females as well as males release gametes into the water, where chance collisions result in fertilized eggs. It's a safe gamble: one female oyster may produce from 10 million to 100 million eggs each year, while males produce several hundred times this amount of sperm. During peak spawning months, the waters of certain bays and inlets are tinged a milky white by the clouds of eggs and sperm from oyster beds.

On their own in the open sea, oyster larvae become part of the plankton community and gradually pass through several developmental stages. After one to three weeks (depending on the species), they are ready to settle on and attach to suitable substrates. Life isn't so rosy for the newly settled oysters, though. Crabs, starfish, marine worms, and other predators love to feed on the youngsters. Disease organisms also threaten the young. Mussels, barnacles, slipper shells, and sponges may compete with them for space and food. Of all those hundreds of thousands of larvae, only a few will attain adulthood. The high incidence of infant oyster mortality is really part of nature's game plan. Former U.S. Bureau of Fisheries scientist Paul Galtsoff once calculated that if all the larvae produced by an eastern oyster were to survive, after three generations, the four- to five-inch-diameter descendants would equal in combined bulk half that of the Earth.

The Birth of Oyster Culture

Who was first to actually cultivate—as opposed to collect—an oyster? It's hard to say when the first experiments in aquaculture began. A frieze from an Egyptian tomb dated 2,000 B.C. hints at the antiquity of fish farming. An ancient Chinese treatise titled *Fish Breeding* suggests that aquaculture was already in a refined state in 475 B.C.

The earliest oyster farmers may have lived in Rome during a time that has been called the Gastronomic Age of Italy, around 100 B.C. Pliny and other historians credit a nobleman named Sergius Orata with first keeping oysters in ponds. Records from that period indicate that Orata was brought to court for turning a pocket of the semi-saline Lake Lucrinus into his personal oyster farm. Orata's lawyer, Lucius Crassus, is said to have warned the prosecution that a court order would not discourage his client from raising oysters. If necessary, Orata would grow oysters on the thatched roof of his home, rather than give up eating oysters.

Orata's efforts at oyster farming may have helped the Romans heat their baths. To warm the water for his oyster broodstock, Orata supposedly mounted a set of pans of oysters on pillars and lit a fire underneath. The hot air circulated beneath the artificial oyster bed. By adjusting the fire, Orata could control the temperature of the water in the pans. It was this innovation, some scholars maintain, that helped the Romans figure out how to heat their baths. It's a good story, but most modern historians don't buy it.

During the Middle Ages, the oyster was a highly prized food, although measures to cultivate it weren't taken. And why would they be, when there were plenty of savory wild oysters to go around? Kings, queens, and commoners ate oysters with style. One English recipe, circa 1390, instructs gourmands to "shell oysters and simmer them in wine and their own broth, strain the broth through a cloth, take blanched almonds, grind them and mix with the same broth and anoint with flour of rice and put the oysters therein, and cast in powder of ginger, sugar, and mace."

The original settlers of North America enjoyed

YES, NORTHWEST OYSTERS HAVE PEARLS

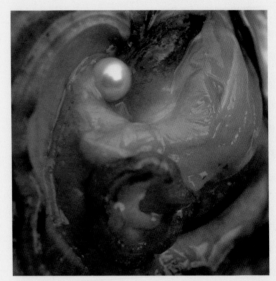

Pearls (above) and pearl shell (right) are prized commodities throughout the world. Pearl culture techniques are credited to Kokichi Mikimoto (1858–1954), pioneer of the Japanese pearl industry.

Pearls are produced by bivalves to isolate and cover any rough-edged and potentially abrasive particles that might insinuate themselves into the shellfish's tenderest parts. A gland in the shellfish's flesh secretes the substance called nacre, which covers the annoying particles, layer upon layer until a pearl is formed.

All bivalves have the potential for making pearls in this fashion, but not every pearl produced is a marketable gem. It's not surprising to find a pearl in a Pacific oyster, but they tend to be odd shaped and dull in color—of inferior quality for fine jewelry.

Japanese pearl oysters (called *akoyagai*) are known the world over for producing high-quality cultured pearls. Techniques for culturing pearls are much more reliable than "playing the odds"—that is, opening hundreds of oysters before finding one pearl. A technician sticks a small, specially formed bead under the farmed oyster's mantle, then sits back and waits while the pearl-making mollusk goes to work. Famous for their lustre are the black pearls made by the black-lipped oyster, *Pinctada margaritafera,* of French Polynesia and the South Seas. These are also commercially cultured. After many years of intensive harvesting, there would be no black-lipped oysters today, if they weren't grown for this purpose.

Of no real commercial value, pearls from Northwest oysters still make charming souvenirs. Workers in shucking houses and oyster bars collect them as curios, sometimes mounting them on stickpins or in rings.

eating the native oysters but did little to rear them. As in Europe, there was no shortage of shellfish back then. Believed to predate the first European colonists, one mound in Maine contains an estimated seven million bushels of discarded oyster shells. By the 17th century, British shellfishers had recognized the importance of conserving their oyster grounds. In 1667, Bishop Thomas Sprat wrote about the British oyster dredgers and how they would use a knife blade to remove young oysters, or "small brood," from empty oyster shells. The dredgers would toss these little oysters so they could grow to "the bigness of an half Crown piece," and in so doing, "preserve the ground for the future."

Japan became an oyster-growing nation long before England or the New World colonies. On a trip to Japan in the 1890s, Bashford Dean uncovered a document from 1708, describing a deal between a Japanese oyster company and a warehouse in Osaka. "From what period, indeed, this oyster-culture has been carried on is not known accurately, but from its present condition, it is evidently the product of centuries," Dean mused.

The idea of oyster aquaculture was slow to reach the West Coast. But when it did in the mid-1800s, it caught fire, consuming the imaginations of hundreds of women and men in the Northwest. By studying the successes and failures of oyster growers worldwide, these fledgling farmers were among the first students of a fairly new discipline—aquacultural science. As the years passed and another generation joined the oystermen's ranks, there were more opportunities to learn. Today, shellfish culture and marketing techniques are shared at colleges and universities, at government- and industry-sponsored workshops and conferences, and in restaurants, community centers, and any other places that oyster growers happen to gather.

AGAIN, THE OYSTERMAN

Which brings us back to the oystermen and why they so willingly devote their lives to shellfish and their beds. Some would say they do it to make a living. Others have a personal connection to the industry—a lineage

Oyster farmer Jeffrey Delia (overleaf) of the Broadspit Oyster Company on Dabob Bay, Washington, is busiest whenever the tide is out. In winter months, this means laboring at night, by the light of a propane-fed flame.

that extends to their grandparents' or great-grandparents' first footseps on a Northwest oyster bed. "What else would I do?" is a frequent answer. In the economically strapped coastal counties where oysters are grown, this question needs no reply.

"Most of the men who engage in oystering are lusty, loyal fellows; a period spent with them is an education in itself," wrote Eldon Griffin. While this portrait was written more than 60 years ago (and unintentionally overlooks women, many of whom are instrumental in keeping the industry strong), it is no less true today. Like the shellfish they plant, tend, and harvest, oyster growers may appear tough on the outside, well protected by a thick, craggy shell. But inside, there's tenderness—and often a pearl of wisdom waiting to be shared.

Some of these pearls have been incorporated in this book. The lessons gleaned from the Northwest oyster industry's 150-year history may guide others—not only aquaculturists, but farmers, foresters, and others engaged in the cultivation of renewable resources—to become better stewards of our fragile planet.

OYSTER CULTURE IN JAPAN

One of the world's first aquacultural endeavors, Japan's oyster industry began centuries ago as an offshoot of an historic fishery for *Venerupis japonica*, the Japanese or Manila clam. Shellfish gatherers collected and held these clams in shallow-water enclosures before taking them to market. Short fences of interlaced bamboo stalks, called *shibi*, ringed the enclosures.

Each stalk's leafy branches were left intact, filling any gaps between bamboo fence posts. As Japan's littleneck harvesters discovered, the leaves and stems of the *shibi* served as collectors, on which the larvae of Pacific oysters could settle and grow. It was soon apparent that greater profits could be realized by cultivating oysters than by gathering and corralling littleneck clams. An industry was born.

Over several centuries, Japanese oystermen refined their growing techniques, first by fastening coarse nets to the semi-submerged bamboo poles (a method known today as hibitate culture) to increase the surface area to which larval oysters could fasten themselves. Even greater yields were realized in the early 1900s, with the adoption of so-called hanging culture techniques. For this innovation, lengths of rope dotted with juvenile oysters were suspended in the shallows of the nation's most productive bays and inlets, thus thwarting crabs, seastars, and other bottom-dwelling predators that might otherwise feed on the sedentary oysters as they grew.

Variations of *shibi*, hibitate, and hanging techniques are still used in 21st-century Japan. These and other advances in oyster culture have bolstered the nation's already strong shellfish industry, with growers producing about 218,000 tons of oyster meat in 1997—nearly 50 times the output of 1920 and four times that of 1941.

The inventors of hanging culture, Japanese oyster farmers tend their shellfish from a fiberglass skiff on a calm sea of floating buoys.

BUYING AND PREPARING OYSTERS

Classic can labels (above) and jar lids (opposite) are sought-after collectibles, especially in prime oyster-growing locales such as Willapa Bay.

If you live in or visit the Pacific Northwest, you should have no problem finding fresh supplies of oysters, regardless of the season or one's proximity to an ocean coast. Large grocery chains routinely keep oysters in stock, as do most seafood markets and many specialty shops. Several kinds of oysters are available, but the most common is the Pacific oyster, described in chapter 4. Many shellfish growers also sell their product directly to the public. Without question, these oysters are the freshest, since they are often harvested the same day they are sold. They may also be the most economical, with no middle man to hike up the retail price.

To purchase live oysters, make sure the shells are undamaged. Fresh oysters should have been out of water no more than 10 days, and they should not be buried in shaved ice. Rather, they should be displayed on top of the ice, with the shell's more rounded, or "cup," side down. Each shell should be closed—a gaping shell means a dead or dying oyster.

Many growers and suppliers also sell shucked oyster meats, already removed from the shell. Shucked oysters are packed in water and their own juices in containers. Look for the pull-date on the container to ensure freshness. Shucked oysters can be frozen up to three months.

Oysters don't take long to cook. However, they should be cooked thoroughly for food safety's sake. Boil or simmer meats for three to five minutes, using small pots so the oysters in the middle are well cooked. Steam live oysters in the shell for four to nine minutes after the shell opens. Discard any unopened shells—there's probably something fishy about these. Broil oysters at least three minutes, three inches from the broiler, or bake them for at least 10 minutes at 450°F.

This book offers a selection of recipes for tasty and

nutritious oyster dishes, some time-honored and straightforward and others more creative in their approaches to haute cuisine. Additional recipes can be obtained from seafood suppliers and, often, from the oyster growers themselves.

There are four more ways to part an oyster from its home:

1. Grill the shells open, following the instructions in this book's recipe for Barbecued Oysters on page 47.

2. Steam them open. First, scrub the shells well. Then put them in a kettle with just enough water to cover the bottom of the pan. Steam until shells open, about five minutes. Lift them out of the pan carefully to avoid spilling any of the liquor, which may be used in many recipes or saved for soup stock and sauces.

3. Heat three or four oysters at a time in a microwave oven for about one minute to make shells easier to pull apart.

4. Hold flat side down on a chopping board and "stab" off the tip end of the shells (farthest from the hinge), and a knife can be easily inserted.

A Few Words about Harvesting from the Wild

Most prime oyster beds in the Pacific Northwest are located on privately owned or leased tidelands. This means that unless you've obtained prior permission from the grower, the oysters in these beds are not for the taking.

In the few sites where the public may harvest oysters, a recreational shellfishing permit from the state or provincial fish and wildlife management agency is probably required. It is also important to consult the local health department for up-to-date information about so-called red tides—seasonal blooms of toxin-producing algae species (described in detail in chapter 6). Should such blooms occur in oyster-growing areas, the shellfish from these beds should not be eaten until the danger has passed.

Minterbrook
OYSTER CO.
Sell By:
0 482046 8
CAUTION: Shell particles may be found in this product, rinse and examine with care before using.
SMALL
10 FL. OZ. (296 ML)
PERISHABLE - KEEP REFRIGERATED

OPENING OYSTERS WITHOUT TEARS

Historically, Northwest oyster shuckers (opposite) opened hundreds of oysters in a day, turning wheelbarrows full of shellfish into buckets filled with tender oyster meats. While workplace conditions are now vastly improved, shucking is still done by hand.

A French engineer recently came up with a way to keep consumers from cutting their hands when opening oyster shells. He calls his invention the pull-tab oyster.

The tab is a flat piece of plastic connected to a loop of stainless steel wire. The wire is threaded around the oyster's adductor muscle, which holds the shell closed. When pulled, it acts like a noose, slicing the muscle. Tug the tab and the oyster falls open. Slow to be accepted by U.S. oyster growers, this technology has been catching on in Japan, France, Belgium, Holland, Ireland, and Canada.

But what should you do with an oyster that has no pull-tab? The following step-by-step instructions are from *Cooking Alaskan* (Alaska Northwest Books), a compendium of more than 1,500 recipes, many of them shellfish-based, from the 49th state. Follow them carefully and you'll be a world-champion oyster shucker in no time.

1. Wear a heavy glove on the hand that holds the oyster. Hold it cupped shell downward, flat shell up, with the hinge pointing toward your wrist.

2. Using an oyster knife or a strong blunt-ended knife with a decent cutting edge, locate the single adductor muscle. It is about two-thirds of the distance from the hinge.

3. Keeping the knife blade pressed against the upper shell, move the knife back and forth until the muscle is severed. Twist the knife to pry off the shell.

4. Probe underneath the oyster to sever the muscle that connects it to the lower shell. Remove the meat or prepare it on the half shell.

Throughout the process, try to preserve as much oyster liquor as you can. Leave it in the shell if the oyster is to be served on the half shell, or strain it to save for other uses.

2. Before the First Farms

We sang as we culled.

—*Cora G. Chase,* The Oyster Was Our World: Life on Oyster Bay 1894 to 1914

Stories about the great gold strike at Sutter's Mill and its aftermath, the rapid invasion of northern California by thousands of prospectors lusting for gold, filled the nation's newspapers in 1848. Little ink was devoted, though, to a second significant strike—the "mining" of a mother lode of oysters in Shoal-Water Bay (today's Willapa Bay), a fertile inlet in the newly charted Washington Territory, 580 nautical miles northwest of the now-legendary mill.

Both events left their marks on the American West. But only the discovery of oysters continues to shape the character, culture, and economies of the Northwest, from California north into coastal Oregon, across Washington, and into British Columbia and southeastern Alaska, the farthest reach of the native oyster's biogeographic realm.

While the gold rush is but remnants relegated to museum collections, historic districts, and tourist attractions, the Northwest oyster industry is still a vital dimension in today's world. More than seven million pounds of oyster meats are harvested each year from well-tended beds in Willapa Bay and in nearby Puget Sound, Washington, supporting an industry

Pacific oyster bins, waiting to be filled (page 26). Self-sufficient prospectors (overleaf) filled the streets of San Francisco (opposite), illustrated in this classic N. Currier print from 1850. The City by the Bay boomed, as did the demand for fresh oysters, during this colorful period in California's history.

valued annually at more than $70 million. Seven million pounds of meat is roughly equivalent to 46 million pounds of oysters in their shells. Annually, this mountain of mollusks puts Washington among the top three oyster-producing states and provinces in North America. Less lucrative but equally important oyster-farming operations bolster the resource-based economies in the other Northwest states and in Canada.

By some accounts, the oyster industry was responsible for the very naming of Washington's state capital. Legend has it that after Washington received statehood in 1889, there was rivalry over where to locate the capital. Olympia had been the territorial capital, but other cities east and west of the Cascade Mountains also put in their claim. The people of Olympia organized a series of public meetings where they presented arguments favoring Olympia as the state capital. The clincher was an oyster dinner served after the meetings that "created a warmth and friendly spirit," in the words of pioneering oysterman E. N. Steele. Olympia won the vote, and from that time on, the local shellfish species was known as the Olympia oyster. While serving as

mayor of Olympia in 1932, Steele issued a proclamation establishing the first week of September as "Oyster Week" in this historic city and throughout the Northwest.

Which, of course, is not to downplay the importance of the gold rush of '49. For it's from this exciting period in U.S. history that the Northwest oyster industry was born.

WORTH THEIR WEIGHT IN GOLD

Only a small percentage of the estimated 200,000 prospectors actually hit pay dirt during the California Gold Rush. The ones who did were all too happy to share their newfound wealth. Many foolhardy miners frittered it away in saloons, casinos, and houses of ill repute. But the Californians who made and more often held on to their fortunes were the service providers: backwoods guides, suppliers of mining equipment, and the owners of hotels, restaurants, and saloons. Among the most successful of these were the oystermen, skilled shellfishers who knew how to mine the invertebrate gold of San Francisco Bay.

Following the Sutter strike, the city of San Francisco boomed, from a town of less than a thousand settlers to a metropolis with more than 30,000 residents.

Dozens of hotels and hundreds of restaurants sprang up, and the proprietors of the new eateries strived in earnest to meet the culinary needs of northern California's nouveau riche.

Meeting those needs required a steady supply of fresh oysters, the official party food of the city's

aurophiles. What better way to announce a gold strike than with a complimentary round of drinks and a few fresh oysters for everyone in the house? It's impossible to know how many of these delicacies were consumed in this way, but it's a good guess that the number approached several million.

"Along with champagne, oysters were the 'symbols of wealth' with which it was customary to celebrate good fortune," offered Joseph R. Conlin in *Bacon, Beans and Galantines: Food and Foodways on the Western Mining Frontier.* Their exorbitant price—a dollar apiece for raw oysters on the half-shell (the same cost as a hen's egg or a slice of bread)—did little to dampen the prospectors' enthusiasm for such rich fare.

Diners across North America shared San Francisco's fondness for oysters in those days, according to Conlin. "While they graced the tables of fine restaurants in large eastern cities, [oysters] were also bolted by the ton in workingmen's saloons (for a penny apiece on the waterfront) and rushed hundreds of miles into the interior even before the railroad," he wrote.

Most of San Francisco's new citizens were from the East Coast, and they carried their cravings for fresh oysters with them into the western wilderness. Oysters remained remarkably popular in temporary miners' camps, far removed from San Francisco and its elite eateries. In most cases, the occupants of these outposts had to settle for tinned shellfish, since the means for transporting fresh foods were not available to them. Where canned goods were hard to obtain, gold miners had to satisfy their cravings with "mock oysters." These poor substitutes for the real thing were made from butter, beaten eggs, and grated green corn.

Brought up on succulent Bluepoint, Cockenoe, and Pemaquid oysters, East Coast émigrés had to adapt to California's smaller, less nectar-filled native species, *Ostrea conchaphila.* In the years before the transcontinental railroad (completed in 1869) linked the two seacoasts, the only way to obtain fresh oysters from the Atlantic Ocean was by ship around Cape Horn or across the Isthmus of Panama—a voyage that took a minimum of six to eight weeks to complete. Few oyster importers could keep their cargo alive for the duration of such a trip. So they did what they could to

A NORTHWEST NATIVE: THE OLYMPIA OYSTER
OSTREA CONCHAPHILA

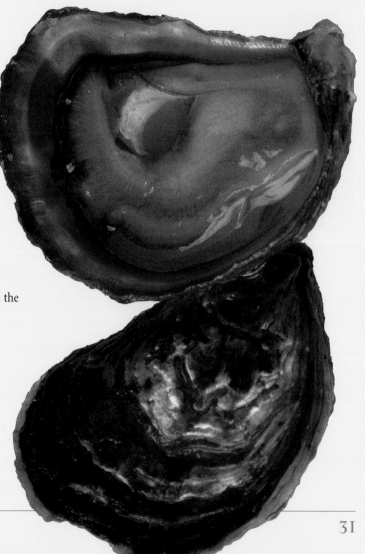

Found in marine waters from Baja California to Sitka, Alaska, the Olympia oyster is the Northwest's only native oyster species. Its small size (less than two inches across) makes this animal easily distinguished from other, nonnative species. "Its shell may be gnarled and eroded, but it does not often show flutings like those on the Japanese oyster," writes University of Washington professor Eugene Kozloff in *Seashore Life of the Northern Pacific Coast.*

Once a common inhabitant of the West Coast's subtidal zone, this species has become increasingly difficult to locate—the silent victim of habitat loss and shoreline degradation from waterfront development. Recreational harvesters of Olympia oysters should focus their searches on the undersides of beach rocks during extremely low tides.

What does an Olympia taste like? Naturalist William Cooper, who traversed the Washington Territory with a team of railroad surveyors in the 1850s, found them to "possess the same peculiar coppery flavor remarked in the European mollusk when eaten for the first time." Today's diners find the slightly metallic aftertaste much to their liking, inspiring a few oyster growers to again try their hand at raising these diminutive delicacies.

31

Tonging was physically taxing, but, as this historic photo reveals, it yielded more oysters in less time than handpicking did.

encourage consumption of local stocks, which at that time were quite plentiful in San Francisco Bay and a few neighboring estuaries.

The Bay's oystermen stood ready to help with this endeavor. Donning hip boots and grabbing pitchforks at low tide—an interval of four to six hours when the water withdraws to reveal the nearshore substrate—they gathered clusters of shells from the exposed rocks and tossed them into bushel baskets, buckets, or gunnysacks. Ambitious pickers could fill four or five bushels in a day, which they'd cart by wheelbarrow or horse-drawn wagon to Bay Area restaurants and fish markets.

To gather oysters when the tidewaters had returned, covering the intertidal sand and mud, or to reach oyster-laden reefs and shoals that were seldom, if ever, exposed to the salt air, San Francisco's oystermen took to canoes and small flat-bottomed skiffs. From these small craft they reaped the Bay's bivalve bounty, using long-handled rakes, called tongs. Hinged at a midpoint like enormous salad servers, these tools were up to 18 feet long. Anything greater than that was too cumbersome to manipulate from a vessel bobbing on

the waves. Their operation was straightforward: an oysterman stood at midpoint of his boat or perched on the gunwales, lowered the tongs into the water, probed the bottom, and when he'd located a good-sized clump of oysters, clamped down with the tongs' teeth, to pry the batch loose. He'd then raise the tongs, passing their length hand over hand. When the tongs were clear of the water, he'd swing them toward the boat, artfully dumping their contents into the center of the boat. He'd repeat this procedure again and again, until his small craft was filled with the sought-after shellfish.

Harvesting with pitchforks and tongs required a second operation—culling—to separate the saleable oysters from the rocks, bits of broken shell, and other debris. Any cracked or broken-shelled specimens were discarded or gobbled on the spot. Such damage prevented the oysters from retaining moisture, greatly reducing their "shelf life." Culling was usually performed on shore, toward the end of a day's work. Often the oystermen hired Native Americans, already well skilled in the art of oyster harvesting, to assist in this endeavor.

Tools of the oyster-tonger's trade are proudly displayed in this historic photograph (left), taken during the late 1800s on central Oregon's Yaquina Bay. Handmade tongs and rakes (above) were fashioned to facilitate easy harvesting of native oysters.

NATIVE TALES...AND THE OYSTER'S TRAVAILS

During a low tide in Jefferson County (opposite), Washington's Scow Bay in the 1880s, members of the S'Klallam tribe forage for Northwest shellfish. Harvesting oysters and clams is still a large part of tribal subsistence. Ambitious aquaculture programs are managed by several Native American groups in Washington, British Columbia, and Alaska.

Oysters are more difficult to collect and prepare than mussels and clams. As such, they probably played a less significant role in sustaining northern California's Native American culture. Nonetheless, the archaeological evidence from the San Francisco Bay area and elsewhere along the Pacific Ocean coast suggests they were an important component of the indigenous people's diets.

The Northwest's First Peoples routinely harvested oysters during low tides of spring and summer. Among the Coast Salish tribes, shellfish gathering was women's work. An individual's prestige was enhanced by her shellfishing abilities. In most instances, the oysters were pried from rocks and other solid substrates by hand, occasionally aided by stones or fire-hardened digging sticks. The meat was removed and often set out to dry for later feasting, and the shells were tossed into piles. At ancient coastal settlements, archaeologists have determined that these huge mounds of discarded oyster shells, called middens, date back at least 3,000 to 4,000 years. Dried oyster meat was reconstituted in fresh water and boiled before being consumed. The thin, flat shells of the oyster's cousin, *Pododesmus cepio*, the jingle shell or rock oyster, were gathered, strung together, and made into rattles and decorations for ceremonial apparel.

Oysters and their kin also figure prominently in Northwest Coast Native American myths and legends. In one creation story, humankind is said to have colonized the planet after escaping from a tightly sealed clam's shell. In another, more lighthearted tale, shellfish are banished to a life in beach sand, after being sentenced by other animals for malicious gossiping. This, the story explains, is why beachwalkers frequently see small spurts of water shooting up from the sand. The clams are trying to clear the silt and seawater they've swallowed while attempting to tell their spiteful tales.

Perhaps the most potent tribal depiction of a native oyster stands at Saxman Village, near Ketchikan, Alaska. Here, at the base of a tall memorial pole, is an oval-shaped carving representing the spirit of a giant oyster. To the side of the oyster, his hand caught in the bivalve's broad, toothy mouth, is the kneeling figure of a man.

Tlingit elder Henry Denny Sr. and his grandchildren gather at the base of the Giant Oyster Totem, a memorial to an unfortunate oyster harvester, in this photograph from 1941 (opposite).

How did a man and a mollusk come to be carved on this pole? Long ago, while hunting at the water's edge, a party of men located an octopus, hidden under a boulder at low tide. While trying to extract the octopus from its den, one of the men reached down and stuck his hand into the crevice beneath the rock. Within seconds, a giant oyster latched onto his wrist. Soon the tide began to return, covering man and oyster with sea water. As the sea began to swallow him, the man started to sing. He continued to sing, even as his head disappeared beneath the waves. When the tide receded, the man's relatives found his corpse washed up on the beach. The man's song was repeated at his funeral and continues to be sung by his descendants, the Giant Oyster house group of the Tlingit people.

Traditional harvest practices by Native Americans did little to diminish the supply of oysters in San Francisco Bay and other shellfish sites. The small number of inhabitants of coastal villages ensured that the impacts of shellfishing would be slight and that oysters would exist for generations to come. All tribal harvesting was conducted with respect, with an eye for maintaining a balance between the needs of humankind and the natural world.

Later European settlers had no such conservation ethic to limit their activities. Their populations were large but not nearly as large as the impacts of over-harvesting. Rather, guided by the concept of Manifest Destiny—a popular philosophy of the mid-1800s that viewed all of nature as a gift from God—they gouged the earth with their mines, carved huge clearcuts into forested hillsides, decimated salmon populations, and consumed other natural resources of the West without a thought for sustainability or the tragic losses later generations would be forced to endure.

"Ages will not exhaust the supply," one overly optimistic reporter for the *New York Tribune* enthused, when assessing California's gold supply in 1849. In a way he was right: 150 years after the fact, lucky hunters can still pluck a few small flakes of gold from wilderness streams. But finding supplies of fresh, edible oysters today is an entirely different story. Within three years of the strike at Sutter's Mill, oyster stocks in San Francisco Bay and smaller embayments had been exhausted.

In hindsight, it's easy to understand how San Francisco shellfishers could have so quickly devastated their oyster beds. To sustain healthy populations, sufficient quantities of mature oysters must be available to breed. By continually reaping without sowing, oyster gatherers made it nearly impossible for even the fecund *O. conchaphila* to naturally restock the bay.

Unwittingly, San Francisco's oystermen also made it difficult for *Ostrea* larvae to mature and reach a harvestable size. To dispose of the calcium-rich remnants of oyster-shucking operations, they often sold the heaps of empty shells to the makers of cement and poultry feed. This shortsighted business practice robbed the free-swimming larval oysters of prime sites of attachment—the shell on which they would eventually settle and start living a sedentary life. Recognizing this fact of life, later oyster growers learned to litter the bottom of their managed oyster beds with the discarded shells—a process known as cultching (and described in chapter 5). With some oyster species, more than 50 of the juveniles, called spat, may settle on a single oyster shell.

The rapid development of San Francisco's urban waterfront may also have played a part in the oysters' sudden disappearance. Undoubtedly, the construction of wharves and other shoreline structures served to muddy the Bay, putting additional stress on any oysters overlooked by the city's overzealous shellfish gatherers.

FINDING FRESH SUPPLIES

Suddenly lacking local stocks, San Francisco's oyster aficionados were now required to search elsewhere for their favorite festive food. And search they did, with help from enterprising shellfish importers. The quest for fresh oysters reached as far south as Mazatlan, 1,400 miles from San Francisco, at the entrance to Mexico's Sea of Cortez. Here, the oysters were "the largest and the best," according to one San Francisco tabloid of the day. Alas, the long transport time and unstable economic conditions in

The large-scale removal of oysters and the stockpiling of empty oyster shells had profound effects on the marine environment. This historic photograph shows an "oyster graveyard" at a now-defunct cement plant on the shores of Puget Sound.

In the 1800s, Willapa Bay was a haven for bivalves, both native and introduced. By 1894, when this map was produced, the bay's best beds had already been staked out and imported eastern oysters had been planted at several choice locales.

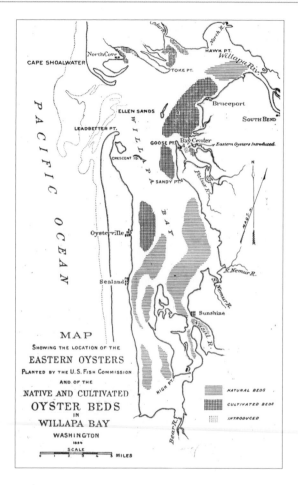

pre-Revolutionary Mexico made importation of shellfish from these distant beds a risky venture at best.

As it turned out, an unrivaled abundance of fresh oysters awaited discovery to the north of San Francisco. With its numerous inlets, sloughs, and tidal channels, Washington Territory's Shoal-Water Bay was a natural haven for bivalves. Nutrient-rich outflow from nearly 1,500 miles of rivers and small streams supported a vast estuarine food web, within which oysters could flourish and multiply. Prairie-like saltmarshes at the mouths of rivers and streams captured any sediment from erosion of the bay's uplands, protecting Shoal-Water's shelled inhabitants from the harmful effects of siltation.

For many generations, the members of the Chehalis, Chinook, and, in more recent times, the Kwalhioqua tribes sustained themselves on Shoal-Water's bounteous shellfish, salmon, shorebird, seabird, and cedar tree resources.

Their lives changed dramatically with the appearance of the first European fur traders and the epidemic diseases they carried. By 1852, when James Gilchrist Swan compiled the notes for his now-classic

C. J. W. RUSSELL'S HOUSE AND INDIAN LODGE.

Far from the posh waterfront dwellings of the Northwest's modern era, the homes of Russell and Chief Toke were local landmarks nonetheless. Many of Shoal-Water's early settlers inhabited even more rustic abodes—simple lean-tos made of rough-hewn timber and sailcloth.

personal chronicle, *Three Years at Shoal-Water Bay*, there were fewer than 120 Chinook people—a tenth of the estimated peak population in pre-contact times. Subsequent explorers stumbled upon a land of unbelievable natural abundance and few people with which to share it.

Among the initial settlers of Shoal-Water's shores was Captain Charles J. W. Russell. In 1850, he built the first European-style house in the region, from which he ran a trading post—an indispensable outlet for his fellow pioneers, most of whom lived in lean-tos of rough-hewn timber roofed with sailcloth. Near Russell's home was the lodge of Chief Toke, leader of the local Chinook Indians. Russell employed many of Toke's tribespeople in what was then a fledgling enterprise—oyster gathering.

"He had a sort of monomania for being called captain, and thinking himself the first discoverer and settler in the Bay," Swan observed. Still, Shoal-Water's early chronicler conceded, "he was a generous fellow at heart, and always exerted himself for the welfare of those in the Bay."

Russell's kindliest act was undoubtedly motivated by self-interest. In November 1851, he traveled south to Astoria, Oregon, boarded a steamboat, and sailed to San Francisco. Here, he introduced the first sacks of Shoal-Water oysters to the city's shellfish merchants.

For this single accomplishment, noted Swan, Russell was now entitled to receive the highest honor that San Francisco could bestow—"a monument of oyster shells to his memory." Shoal-Water's residents had reason to erect a similar edifice, as did citizens throughout Washington, Oregon, and British Columbia. For thanks to Russell, one of the more lucrative ventures of the 19th-century Northwest had been launched.

SHOAL-WATER SHELLFISH FOR SALE

Russell's sacks represented the tip of an oyster iceberg. Over the years, a virtual flotilla of schooners arrived at Shoal-Water Bay, brought aboard bushels of wild-harvested oysters, and then made haste for San Francisco, where jubilant diners awaited.

The same schooners loaded their holds with lumber—the raw materials for building California's boom towns—from sawmills in Astoria and other coastal communities. Still, they had plenty of deck space to fill with oyster bushels, barrels, and crates. "Schooners can carry from 1,200 to 2,000 baskets of oysters and some have even taken 4,000 baskets (but that is not considered safe to take so many at once, as the bottom ones are apt to die on the passage)," Swan reported.

Similar trade routes were later established in Netarts and Yaquina Bays in the Oregon Territory, as well as in Olympia, at the southernmost end of Washington's Puget Sound. Nonetheless, nearly

90 percent of all of San Francisco's imported oysters came from the bay we now know as Willapa, so the business became known as "the Shoal-Water Bay trade."

By 1855, at the end of Swan's stint at Shoal-Water, there were 28 boats, 21 scows, 13 canoes, and one 20-ton schooner in operation. Swan calculated that these vessels could collectively transport a total of 5,450 baskets—about 10 percent of the volume of oysters leaving the bay every year. "When the schooner was secured, an oyster boat would come along each side of her, the oystermen scooping their wares into schooner baskets which were passed up to the ship," recalled Emerson J. Watson, a second-generation Willapa resident. "As soon as one boat was unloaded, it would drop back to allow another to take its place."

As in gold rush towns, Willapa's oysters were worth their weight in gold, the currency most often exchanged between schooner operators and oystermen, according to Watson:

Father said that many times when he landed on the beach at Bruceport, he would see a group of men pitching twenty dollar gold pieces at a marker set up in the sand, the one coming the closest taking the pot. Father never gambled … so even though he had a large family, he saved a considerable number of those gold pieces. There were no banks, so it was a case of putting money away in a safe, secret place.

The same basket that cost $1 at the source could command $30 at San Francisco's wholesale seafood markets. The wholesale price was then doubled by the owners of restaurants and retail shops. No wonder Washington's shellfish beds had such appeal with ship owners. One schooner captain, Thomas J. Foster, is said to have sailed between San Francisco and Shoal-Water 74 times from 1875 to 1880—on average, a trip every 25 days.

Their holds filled with timber and decks occupied by oyster mounds, Northwest schooners left Shoal-Water Bay bound for San Francisco—and thousands of oyster connoisseurs.

THOSE "NOBLE-HEARTED OYSTERBOYS"

Poised in Native dugout canoes, Shoal-Water Bay's residents wait for the tide to turn in this illustration (opposite) from James Swan's book *The Northwest Coast*, published in 1857.

Oyster growers are a special breed, especially in the Pacific Northwest. Hardworking, loyal, and often generous beyond measure, they've set standards for community spirit, even in the formative days of the oyster industry.

"The early settlers…were some of the most hospitable men that could be found in any part of the world," James Swan observed in *Three Years at Shoal-Water Bay*. "Their isolated position, far from any other settlement…seemed to knit them together in a common bond of brotherhood, and each seemed to vie with the other in acts of kindness to every stranger that might visit the Bay, either from motives of curiosity or to become permanent settlers."

Sometimes that spirit was stretched to its limits. Still, kindness and charity reigned among Shoal-Water's settlers, according to Swan. "The winter of 1852–53 was a hard one for the oystermen," he wrote. "They had supplied themselves, as they supposed, with sufficient provisions for the winter, but the unusual calls on their hospitality from new-comers strained their means so that they were reduced to pretty short allowances; but they did not complain. Those that had not an abundance were cheerfully supplied by those that had, and as there appeared to be a sort of pride that no stranger should suppose them in want, they managed to change and shift their commodities so as to get through the winter without any difficulty…. Their hospitality was the theme of remark all over the Territory, and the oyster-boys of Shoal-Water Bay were looked upon as a community of generous and noble-hearted men."

A Prospector's Repast

Perhaps the best known of oyster dishes associated with the gold rush days is Hangtown Fry. Several stories have circulated surrounding the origin of this dish. Richard Conlin and other gold rush historians offer this scenario: that in Hangtown, the original name of Placerville, California, a forty-niner may have requested the most expensive dish in the house. The cook at this establishment promptly met this request, scrambling eggs with some onions and folding in oysters. Since many cooks in those times were Chinese, it's possible that Hangtown Fry was really nothing more than a fancified egg foo yong, an Americanized element of Cantonese cuisine.

Hangtown Fry

Drain and pat dry 2 dozen medium-sized California oysters, season them with salt and pepper, and roll first in flour, then in beaten egg, and then in fine white bread crumbs. Put them into a hot frying pan with melted butter, and fry to a golden brown on one side; before turning them over, pour over all 4 or 5 whole eggs beaten lightly. Let cook a minute, then turn over and brown on the other side to color them just as desired. The resulting dish will look like an egg pancake with oysters mixed in. Serve with 2 or 3 links of tiny browned breakfast sausages and shoestring potatoes.

(From: *Consider the Oyster* by M. F. K. Fisher. North Point Press, New York, 1954)

THE FIRST PEOPLE'S FEAST

Ready to sample the indigenous cuisine of the Pacific Northwest? The Coast Salish tribes—the first settlers of Washington's Willapa Bay and Puget Sound country—used two methods to prepare the native Olympia oyster for feeding guests at potlatches and other social gatherings.

BARBECUED OYSTERS

Build a beach fire with alder, cherry, apple, or any slow-burning wood. Let it burn to glowing coals. Place the oysters on the coals. Make sure that all are tightly closed. The oysters will sputter and steam. When they are baked, the shells will open. Eat immediately, as is, from the half shell.

STEAMED OYSTERS

For this method, the Salish people dug a shallow trench and layered the bottom with igneous rocks. They started a fire over the rocks using cedar tinder and kindling, and slowly added the wood. Alder wood was preferred for steady heat and smoky flavor. It took hours to achieve the right intensity of heat. When ready, the glowing coals were raked aside, the food covered and placed on top of the rocks, and the coals raked back over to cook.

After building a pit fire, place a layer of seaweed on the coals, lay the oysters on the seaweed, and cover them with more seaweed. Heap rocks and gravel on top to a depth of a foot or more. Allow the pit fire to remain for up to an hour. Test for doneness by digging into one corner of the pit. Use tongs to remove an oyster. The oyster is done if the shell is open.

(From: *The Feast is Rich: A Guide to Traditional Coast Salish Indian Food Gathering and Preparation* by Carol Batdorf. Whatcom Museum of History and Art, Bellingham, Washington, 1980)

Easy to prepare and serve, barbecued oysters are natural crowd-pleasers at picnics, fairs, and festivals (opposite). The contents of 10-ounce jars (below) are equally appealing and can be incorporated in a wide range of dishes.

47

Perhaps the oldest oyster can label on record, this one (below, right) includes directions for making a simple oyster stew.

If you're cooking on a home grill rather than a beach fire, you might try the techniques suggested in the *Pike Place Public Market Seafood Cookbook*.

BARBECUED OYSTERS

Preheat the barbecue or grill. Place scrubbed in-shell oysters on the grill rack about 4 inches from the heat. Be sure the oysters are rounded-side down so they cook in their own juices. If using a barbecue with a hood, lower the hood. If using a grill, loosely cover the oysters with a tent of aluminum foil. Cook for 7 to 15 minutes, depending on the size of the oysters. Do not turn the oysters during cooking. Shells may open slightly when oysters are done, but not always. Look for steam or bubbles around the fluted edges of the shell as a signal that oysters are ready. Carefully lift off the top shell and enjoy.

(From: *Pike Place Public Market Seafood Cookbook* by Braiden Rex-Johnson. Ten Speed Press, Berkeley, California, 1997)

PARTY FOR THE PILGRIMS

Oyster stuffing for the Thanksgiving or Christmas turkey has been a tradition in North American families from coast to coast, probably since the days of the first colonial settlers. On the West Coast, the Olympia oyster was known to give a favorite recipe its remarkable character. As one grower of this particular species says, the Olympia oyster is "the tiniest, tastiest morsel of seafood known to man."

In the late 1890s, when it became popular to publish and sell cookbooks for charity, the church groups and women of the Northwest did not miss the opportunity to promote these local delights. They submitted their favorite recipes for all to enjoy. This one comes from Pomeroy, Washington, 1904.

OYSTER DRESSING FOR TURKEY OR CHICKEN

Take a loaf of bread (trimmed of crust); cut into small squares with sharp knife. Sprinkle with salt, pepper, and sage to taste. Dissolve in 1 pint of liquor from the fowl, 3 tablespoons of butter. Pour over the bread. Add 1 can of fresh or cove oysters. Stir with a fork, just enough to distribute the oysters evenly through the bread. Add the whites of 5 eggs beaten to a stiff froth. Stir this lightly through the mixture and bake 40 minutes.

(From: *The Way We Ate: Pacific Northwest Cooking, 1843–1900* by Jacqueline B. Williams. Washington State University Press, Pullman, 1996)

For a more modern version of stuffing, try Chef Eric Jenkins' recipe, which follows:

OYSTER STUFFING

1/4 cup butter	1/4 cup chopped parsley
2 small onions, chopped	6 to 8 cups bread cubes
1 bunch celery, chopped	1 tablespoon ground sage
1 tablespoon chopped garlic	1 tablespoon dried thyme
4 cups chicken stock	Salt and pepper
1 quart shucked oysters, halved if large, liquor reserved	1 cup grated Parmesan cheese

Heat the butter in a large saucepan over medium heat and saute the onions, celery, and garlic for about 5 minutes or until limp. Add chicken stock and oyster liquor. Boil to reduce by one-third, then add the oysters and the parsley. Return just to a boil, then immediately take the pan from the heat. Add the bread crumbs, enough to make a moist dressing but not wet. Add the sage, thyme, and salt and pepper to taste, then stir in the Parmesan cheese. Put the stuffing in a large, buttered baking dish and bake at 350° F until heated through and somewhat crusty on the top and sides, 15 to 20 minutes. Makes about 10 cups.

(From: Chef Eric Jenkins, Duncan Law Seafood Consumer Center, Astoria, Oregon, 2000)

3. COLLECTORS BECOME CULTIVATORS

When the tide is out, there is set in Willapa harbor a table 24 miles long ... and it might be added that the viand is served in only one style—in the shell.

—*"Pacific Coast Oyster Growing,"* The Fishing Gazette, *April 13, 1912*

Word of Shoal-Water Bay, with its seemingly endless supply of oysters waiting to be plucked, spread rapidly up and down the coast. By now, claims to the bay's more productive tidelands had already been staked, so later settlers to the Northwest had to look elsewhere for sources of shelled gold.

Some were fortunate, finding good sites in southern Puget Sound—Mud Bay, Skookum Inlet, and the aptly named Oyster Bay near present-day Olympia. Other homesteaders capitalized on the bivalve bonanza in tide-swept Hood Canal, the geographically isolated San Juan Islands, and the protected northern waters of Samish and Bellingham Bays.

Unlike Shoal-Water, though, there was no schooner traffic serving these largely unsettled corners of the Northwest. As such, the greatest customers for oysters were fellow pioneers, recently arrived and anxious to replenish any food stores they'd exhausted during the arduous treks overland to the Washington and Oregon Territories.

Of course, there were exceptions. In January 1852, the schooner *Juliet* was caught in a squall and driven ashore, midway along the coast of Oregon. Here the ship's captain discovered a navigable river, the Yaquina, whose shores were lined with tall conifers and whose

Harvesting by hand (opposite). An antique Japanese bill of sale (above), proof that oysters were imported to Washington as long ago as 1904.

Northwest shucking houses were hubs of activity in the 1800s. Carved into the back wall of this Oregon facility (opposite) are the words Oysterville and San Francisco, plus the initials of shuckers who worked at this place.

channels abounded with oysters and clams. His find prompted others to settle near the mouth of the river, a convenient spot for serving the many San Francisco-based schooners hauling lumber from nearby sawmills.

"A handsome little town is just beginning on Yaquina Bay," reported the *Oregonian* newspaper, 12 years after the *Juliet*'s grounding. "The principal trade now is in oysters with the San Francisco market." Yaquina's oysters, the *Oregonian* later claimed, were "about double the size of the Puget Sound oyster." Apparently they were nowhere nearly as abundant: by the late 1880s, overharvesting had caused Yaquina's native oysters to disappear.

Yaquina was one of several Northwest towns founded in the mid-1800s on mounds of sun-bleached oyster shells. As Shoal-Water's business continued to boom, settlements such as Oysterville, Bruceport, Bay Center, and Diamond City blossomed. The most northerly community on Washington's Long Beach Peninsula, Oysterville was founded in 1854 by lumberman Robert H. Espy and his partner Isaac A. Clark, a tailor from New York who'd made a modest

fortune during the California gold rush. The pair arrived in a leaky canoe, "borrowed," legend has it, from an Indian graveyard. Lost in the fog, they were guided to prime oyster grounds by Chief Nahcati. It's said that, after hearing the splash of their paddles, Nahcati called Espy and Clark ashore by beating on a hollow log. The newcomers named their settlement Oysterville. Thirty years later, the neighboring town of Nahcotta was named for the helpful chief.

At the height of the native oyster mania, Oysterville possessed more gold per capita than any other town or city along the Pacific Coast, with the sole exception of San Francisco. According to local lore, the nearest bank was in Astoria, so much of the gold was either lost in transit or buried in the sand around Oysterville. Despite numerous treasure-hunters' attempts, no such wealth has ever been recovered.

Bruceport was named for the schooner *Robert Bruce*, whose crew begrudgingly became the first permanent settlers of Shoal-Water Bay. For reasons that remain unclear, the ship's devious cook set the *Robert Bruce* on fire in 1851, forcing the survivors to build a communal

On the Atlantic coast of North America, eastern oysters were so plentiful in the late 1700s that people of all ages and incomes could enjoy them (opposite). As human populations grew and oyster supplies dwindled in the early 1800s, only well-to-do diners could afford these treats.

lodge called Bruce Boys Camp on the shore opposite the charred vessel.

Bay Center got its name because of its location, midway along Shoal-Water Bay—not for its role as a hub of human activity. A community of shanties and shacks, Diamond City was abandoned in the early 1870s, after local supplies of oysters were depleted by its residents—about 75 bachelors who'd bought tideland from San Francisco speculator Isaac Doane. In its heyday, this historic oystering locale is said to have glittered like diamonds when the setting sun struck its mounds of empty oyster shells, hence its inspirational name.

EAST MEETS WEST

Northern California's oystermen had no intention of letting their lucrative business slip into Washingtonians' hands. Green with envy, they watched the ships from Shoal-Water unload their wares and schemed of ways to rebuild the oyster stocks of San Francisco Bay. Assisted

by the Union–Central Pacific transcontinental railroad, they made their move, calling for reinforcements in the form of eastern oysters (*Crassostrea virginica*) from New England, some 3,000 miles away.

Since colonial times, residents of five New England states—New Hampshire, Massachusetts, Rhode Island, Connecticut, and New York—had been enjoying the natural bounty of eastern oysters. Like San Francisco's and Shoal-Water's workers, they relied primarily on tonging from rowboats and dugout canoes. By the mid-1700s, when their oysters became scarce because of overfishing and habitat degradation, these early harvesters started laboring farther from shore, using huge, mechanical dredges to haul up oysters from heretofore inaccessible reefs, 20 or more feet beyond the reach of the lowest tides.

Scooping giant dredgeloads of oysters had even more disastrous effects on the already diminished local stocks. In 1766, it prompted the Assembly of East Greenwich, Rhode Island, to pass an act "forbidding dredging or other methods of taking oysters except tonging."

Rather than abandon the depleted beds, oystermen at the dawn of the 19th century started "planting" the grounds with immature oysters from then-productive Chesapeake Bay. This process of planting and harvesting oysters in well-tended beds marked the real beginning of oyster farming in North America. By 1820, eastern oyster growing operations were firmly established in all five states. Scores of packinghouses, employing hundreds of men, women, and children, and numerous peripheral businesses—from boatyards to blacksmith shops—were born in the process.

Most of California's prospectors had come from "Back East" and were wistfully aware of the abundance of fleshy and flavorful oysters they'd left behind. Imagine their delight when the October 22, 1869, issue of the San Francisco tabloid, *Alta California*, announced that "The first carload of Baltimore and New York oysters in shells, cans, kegs, all in splendid order, has arrived, packed and shipped by the pioneer oyster house of the west, A. Booth, Chicago, Ill."

That carload and subsequent shipments came by way of the Union–Central Pacific railroad. Linking New York with San Francisco, the rail line could deliver live shellfish

from the East Coast in about 18 days. While considerably faster than a boat ride around Cape Horn, the trip was still an ordeal for adult oysters, three-quarters of which perished en route. In transit, the oysters were covered with straw mats. The mats had to be kept damp or the oysters would dry out. If the mats were too wet, though, the oysters would open their shells—a reflex that caused them to dehydrate and die. The fortunate few that endured the overland journey were hastily planted in beds, initially located on the southern shore of San Francisco Bay. At these sites, the introduced mollusks could acclimate and, if all went well, fatten a bit before being brought to market.

OYSTER ENEMIES, NATIVE AND INTRODUCED

California's first oyster cultivators learned the hard way that many imported eastern oysters would not reach a harvestable age. A portion of the transplants died of delayed stress within a few weeks of being placed in their new beds. Others were devoured on site by the Bay's predatory bat rays. Close relatives of sharks and skates, bat rays are large bottom-dwelling fish with big bovine heads and broad, triangular "wings"—fins made of cartilage, nearly six feet across. They prowl the sea floor, searching for snails, crabs, and other marine invertebrates, including oysters and clams, on which to dine. By flapping their wings to create a disturbance, they expose these small delicacies buried beneath the sand. To combat such depredations, San Francisco's shellfish growers were forced to build fences of close-set stakes, driven into the mud to keep the rays from gaining access and gobbling their profits.

A small snail, *Urosalpinx cinerara*, proved an even greater menace to oyster production in the San Francisco area. However, in this case, the oyster importers only had themselves to blame: these small, spiral-shelled pests were dumped into California's waters along with shipments of oysters and other shellfish they feed on. As its common name implies, the eastern drill comes equipped with a rasping tongue to wear a small

INTRODUCING THE EASTERN OYSTER
CRASSOSTREA VIRGINICA

Also known as Gulf, Atlantic, or American oysters, easterns are popularity prize winners at seafood bars on both U.S. coasts. With a thick, deeply cupped and elongated shell (two to five inches across), this East Coast bivalve is both well proportioned *and* tasty. "They surpass those in England by far in size, indeed they are four times as large," Michel, a New World adventurer, wrote in 1701. "I often cut them in two before I could put them in my mouth."

Eastern oysters thrive on reefs in water depths of between 8 and 25 feet. They were once so plentiful in East Coast embayments that they posed navigational hazards to ships. However, the effects of disease and habitat destruction have caused many populations to dwindle dramatically. In Chesapeake Bay, for example, eastern oysters have been reduced to 1 percent of their former abundance. Recent observations indicate the bay's oysters may be staging a comeback.

Today, this species is grown commercially along the Atlantic seaboard and in the Gulf of Mexico. Its many "trade" names—Appalachicola, Blue Point, Cape Cod, and Chincoteague to name but a few—pinpoint the regions from which these oysters were harvested. Several Northwest growers also cultivate eastern oysters, without giving them region-specific monikers.

Bat rays (right) raised a ruckus in San Francisco Bay before oystermen built fences to keep them from beds of eastern oysters. Other biological threats were more difficult to exclude. Thick mats of *Spartina alterniflora* (opposite) now fringe much of Willapa Bay. This introduced species of cordgrass has threatened to crowd out native plant species and make life miserable for shellfish growers in this and other Northwest bays.

hole in the oyster's otherwise impervious shell. Having gained access to the oyster's soft interior, the $1\frac{1}{2}$-inch-long drill inserts its skinny proboscis into the hole and slurps the meat.

The eastern drills had no natural enemies to limit their spread, so they quickly overran some of the oyster-growing locales in south San Francisco Bay. Unable to curb their numbers by hand-picking, oyster growers resorted to starving the drills, refraining from planting any additional oysters in the most heavily infested beds. Despite their efforts, the drills remain pestiferous in Tomales Bay and other places to this day. A regular Noah's Ark of East Coast snails, shrimp, crabs, and worms have also found life in the Bay to their liking.

Eastern oyster growers have been blamed for introducing yet another, perhaps more devastating organism to the Northwest. The culprit in this case is not an animal but a plant—the nonnative *Spartina alterniflora*, or smooth cordgrass. It's been theorized that this fast-growing marsh plant was once used as packing in the freight cars carrying crates and barrels of eastern oysters. When these shipments were unloaded on the waterfront, it's possible that smooth cordgrass seeds and cuttings were dumped on the ground, then carried by breezes or water currents, establishing isolated clumps on the mudflats of Shoal-Water and other bays.

With neither natural predators nor plant competitors to thwart its growth, *Spartina* rapidly expanded its range. At first, the clumps of the reedy grass were barely noticed. But as the years passed, it became harder to overlook the fact that the bay's topography was changing. Silt from shoreline erosion was being captured by the cordgrass' roots, shoots, and stalks. In this way, oyster growing areas were being transformed into grassy cordgrass meadows.

Because *Spartina* has little food or habitat value, its presence adversely affects many other forms of life. Migratory seabirds and shorebirds use coastal estuaries as rest stops in their seasonal flights to and from Mexico. *Spartina*'s rapid encroachment (expanding its mass by about 20 percent per year in some locales) has greatly reduced the acreage available to these long-distance fliers, possibly taking an irreversible toll on bird populations.

Today *Spartina* is the target of eradication efforts by federal, state, and local agencies, and interest groups. Resource managers have tried mowing, handpicking, spraying with herbicides and, most recently, releasing an aphid-like insect, *Prokelisia marginata*, that feeds exclusively on *Spartina* stems. To date, none of these methods has proven effective against the Plant Kingdom's answer to Attila the Hun.

SEEDING AN IDEA:
WASHINGTON'S OYSTER RESERVES

Prime shellfish locales are worth preserving. A system of reserves helps ensure that oysters will reseed themselves.

By 1918, when Washington's oyster growers shipped fewer than 1,000 bushels of oysters to market, legislators knew it was time to act. Oystermen had worked hard to supply California's demand for oyster meats, but because the shell needed for the growth of new oysters had been shipped out of state as well, lack of new crops threatened to terminate the state's lucrative oyster industry.

The state's lawmakers had a grand plan for halting the decimation of oyster stocks. Because of the Callow Act, shellfish growers were already being allowed to purchase the lands they had been cultivating. What if the state set aside a few thousand acres of prime oyster-growing land, called "reserves," where the Department of Fisheries would maintain a ready supply of oyster seed? Then growers would always have the means to restock their own tidelands. They would pay a small fee to help maintain the reserves, and the industry would be saved.

The system worked for a while, most notably in Puget Sound's Oakland Bay, where Olympia oyster seed naturally flourished. But in 1927 the system failed: for unexplained reasons, the oysters in their state-protected beds did not grow, and successive efforts could not restore productivity to the bay. Other reserves were depleted, and the state was left with tidelands that could not be sold or cultivated in competition with the shellfish industry.

Washington's dependence on oyster reserves has declined in recent years. At the same time, interest in recreational shellfish harvesting has increased, as has the commercial value of clams, reviving the idea that reserves are a grand way to provide public access to these delectable resources.

GROWING, GROWING

As eastern oyster culture evolved, importers shifted their efforts from fattening the adult specimens to raising juveniles from the shores of New York—principally Newark and Raritan Bays, and the Hudson and Raritan Rivers. Three-inch-long juveniles had easier times riding the rails and were much less expensive to transport en masse. They went for about $5 per barrel, with as many as 8,000 individuals crammed into one of these stout wooden casks. The youngsters were spread out on the very beds once occupied by Northwest native oysters and, with limited protection from predators and poachers, allowed to feed and fend for themselves for two to four years. The first experimental plantings of one- and two-year-old eastern oysters proved promising. In San Francisco Bay's comparatively warmer waters, the oysters grew year-round, attaining a marketable size nearly a year earlier than on the East Coast.

It is nearly impossible to assess the annual output of eastern oysters during their first years of importation. Growers seldom reported production figures, and when they did, they listed pounds, gallons, bushels, barrels, shucked meats, shells, and other inconsistent measures. Better records were kept by East Coast oyster shippers, who between 1887 and 1900 transported an average of 124 freight car loads of juvenile eastern oysters to San Francisco each year. With approximately 270 bushels per carload, California's importers deposited about 33,480 bushels of oysters annually—that's more than 90 bushels per day—into their bay. During those glory years, eastern oyster culture accounted for 80 percent of the total oyster production in San Francisco Bay.

Meanwhile, in Washington, growers were making sure that their cash crop of native oysters, now dubbed "Olympias" in recognition of the new state capital, would remain ever abundant. They began diking the tidelands, laying down logs and lumber to impound the seawater as the tide ebbed. Such modifications of the shoreline served two purposes. First, the diked areas allowed stockpiling of surplus oysters gathered during previous low tides or under more favorable weather conditions. Second, they made it easier for the farmers to keep tabs on their stock and to guard against

The place where the cut was to be made would be marked by stakes when the tide was out. When the tide came in, floats would be brought and set in place by the use of anchor poles thrust into the bottom. When the tide went out again, workmen, using what was known as a mud fork dug down to the desired depth and loaded the floats. On the high tide, this oyster mud would be floated out to the area to be filled behind the dike.

The newly made dikes were then lined with gravel, a foot or two deep, creating commodious, silt-free beds in which the native oysters could grow. Some oystermen favored a floor of wood planks for their dikes. These were replaced in later years by dikes constructed of cement.

Constructing dikes was one thing; getting oysters to thrive in them was another. Many tales of personal hardship have been told by the early oyster growers, but few can surpass John Joseph Brenner's. Born in Wisconsin in 1860, Brenner moved west at age 21, first working as a laborer for the Canadian Pacific Railroad

By constructing dikes in the intertidal zone (above), Northwest oyster farmers could greatly enhance the productivity of their beds. However, the extra cost of construction meant growers (opposite) had even more at stake.

encroachments by seastars and other oyster predators.

Landowners also took to grading their oyster beds, leveling the beach behind the dikes to make more uniformly productive substrates for growing. Often, leveling meant adding fill substrate, usually gravel outwash from river mouths, to diked areas—a tricky and time-consuming operation.

"To do this, log floats would be used," explained oysterman E. N. Steele, founder of Washington's Rock Point Oyster Company, in *The Rise and Decline of the Olympia Oyster*:

The J. J. Brenner Oyster Company of Olympia, Washington (opposite), grew rapidly in the 1920s. In the spring of 1927, its operations were moved to a two-story facility with separate rooms for shucking, refrigerating, and packing shellfish.

and then as a logger in Olympia, Washington. After a brief foray as a dairyman, he purchased a tract of oyster lands from the Indians for $30 an acre. Returning to examine his land at low tide, he found the newly acquired oyster beds in a sadly depleted state. He traded his sole possession, an old horse, for eight floatloads of oysters, with which he replanted his beds. Since he and his family lived in Olympia, 6 miles from the tidelands, he was required to trek 12 miles on foot each day. While waiting for the beds to rebuild, Brenner took a job in Seattle for what was then considered the minimum wage—14 cents an hour. After an absence of four years, he returned to Olympia and his oyster beds, working each day from dawn until dusk. Brenner's persistence paid off, and in 1893 he founded the J. J. Brenner Oyster Company in Olympia. Money from this large-scale operation allowed him to buy additional oyster acreage and build a fine home on the west shore of Olympia's Mud Bay. Brenner's descendants remain in the oyster business to this day.

Despite their efforts to cultivate even more oyster-friendly lands, many of Washington's oystermen would soon find themselves in financially dire straits. The popularity of the eastern oyster had caused the price of their Olympia oysters to come crashing down. Before the completion of the transcontinental railroad, San Francisco's buyers were offering $16 for a sack of a thousand of these oysters. By the mid-1870s, the price of "Olys" had dipped to a mere $4 a sack. Ten years later, the same sack fetched $2.50—about half the price paid for the esteemed easterns. The once-lucrative Olympia oyster industry was now as lifeless as a sun-bleached oyster shell.

For Washingtonians, getting in on the eastern action meant completing their own spur of the transcontinental railroad, the Northern Pacific Railway line. Tracks of this light-gauge railroad would connect the small towns around Shoal-Water Bay with Kalama on the Columbia River, already linked to Tacoma on the eastern shore of Puget Sound. From this point, the mainline ran east, over the Cascade Mountains to a terminus at Lake Superior, then on to the East Coast with its money-making eastern oyster supplies.

Construction of this network began in 1870—a year

after San Francisco's settlers started slurping down imported Blue Point oysters with zeal. Alas, financial troubles and other woes prevented the Northern Pacific's builders from finishing their project for another 23 years. In 1894, the same year that the first carload of Washington apples was shipped out-of-state, the U.S. Fish Commission purchased 80 barrels of eastern oysters, planting them in the channel of the Palux River at Bay Center, the approximate midpoint of Shoal-Water Bay.

"Unfortunately, however, the place selected for this experiment seems to have been a poor one," suggested the Washington

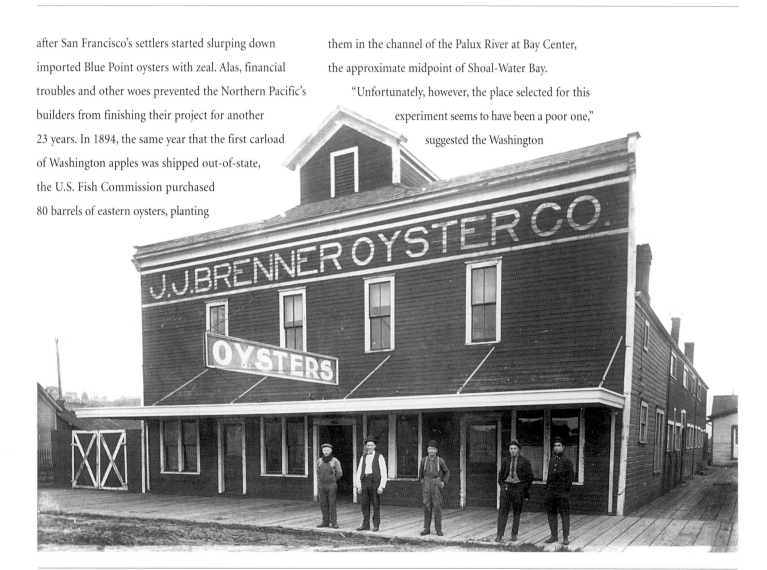

Agricultural College's R. W. Doane in his 1901 report to the state fish commissioner. Although "quite a number of the oysters were found there a year or more after they were planted," Doane confessed, "the channel began to change and the oysters were soon all buried in the mud."

Five years later, the fish commissioner's staff tried a similar experiment, in a more welcoming spot. With a $7,500 appropriation from the Washington State Legislature, they purchased an assortment pack of eastern oysters—78 barrels from coastal Connecticut, 9 from Chesapeake Bay, 18 from New York's East River, and 10 each from Massachusetts and Maryland's Princess Bay. The oysters were packed in well-ventilated barrels and shipped in a refrigerator car, which was re-iced at least once along the way. The car left Fair Haven, New York, on April 11 and reached Tacoma on April 23. From there, the barrels were taken by a steamer, some to Tokeland, a few miles due north of Bay Center, and the rest to Keyport, at the entrance to Liberty Bay on Puget Sound. By the next afternoon, the oysters had settled in their beds and, shells agape, were making up for lost time, busily filter-feeding after a fast of 12 days.

AN EASTERN EMPIRE

Two months later, many of the oysters from Connecticut had ripened, their gonads full of eggs or sperm. The Chesapeake oysters ripened next, "with the rest following suit," according to Doane.

Encouraged by the early signs that Washington's oyster transplants had adapted to their new surroundings, fisheries managers began speculating about rearing other foreign delicacies in Northwest bays and inlets. Today, the notion of adding a nonnative organism to an ecosystem without a thorough investigation of the introduction's potentially harmful effects would cause conservation biologists to cringe. But in the late 1800s, the importance of such preliminary studies had yet to be realized. "Certainly everything should be done that can be done to fill our waters with good varieties of any class of fish that might do well here," enthused Doane, calling for the large-scale importation of lobsters and crayfish into Shoal-Water Bay. Doane also proposed that a second nonnative oyster, the Japanese or Pacific oyster (*Crassostrea gigas*) be cultivated in this fertile home away from home.

Doane's cries for exotic crustaceans went unheeded by all but a few adventurous aquaculturists, who eventually tried the Japanese oysters. In 1899, the state fish commissioner contacted a Professor Mitsukari of the Imperial University of Tokyo, who later helped obtain a few batches of live stock from Japan's northernmost island, Hokkaido, for plantings in Puget Sound. A few years later, a group of Japanese immigrants tried to replicate this feat, purchasing another small shipment for their beds near Bellingham, Washington. For reasons presented in the next chapter, neither attempt was successful at bearing "fruit" from the sea.

Alternatively, rearing eastern oysters in Washington was a cinch—or so it seemed. One only needed to buy baby oysters from afar, plant them, and wait for the comestibles to come of age. No sooner had state workers established the feasibility of such ventures than private oyster growers tried their hands at it. The first commercially important planting was made in 1899, by the Toke Point Oyster Company of South Bend, which went so far as to copyright its locally reared shellfish,

using the name of Russell's neighbor, Chief Toke, as a trademark.

Within a decade, the Washington business in eastern oysters had burgeoned into an enterprise valued at around $1 million and employing several hundred individuals. Production figures steadily climbed from about 4,000 gallons of meat in 1902 to 20,000 gallons in 1908. "Many will remember and smile at the great interest, not to say excitement, manifested over the shipment of 80 barrels of eastern oysters to this bay in 1895, while now the importation of from 50 to

Tales of daily life in Willapa Bay's picturesque early station houses still circulate today. At one time, there were eight of these "wooden islands"—a descriptive phrase coined by oysterman Harlan Herrold.

Barrels of eastern oysters were loaded onto the *Bay Point* (opposite), which ferried them to growing sites offshore. A well-appointed dredge boat, the *Bay Point* was built in South Bend, Washington, in 1907 and is still operating today.

100 carloads annually excites little comment," a 1906 issue of South Bend's *Willapa Harbor Pilot* newspaper observed.

Oregonians also tried to raise eastern oysters, to a far lesser extent than their neighbors to the north. A few British Columbia growers also entered the market. And of course, California's oyster harvesters kept themselves busy, supplying eastern oysters to local diners. Some of California's best customers happened to be Shoal-Water growers, who paid handsomely for any extra easterns they might add to their beds.

Along with eastern oyster culture came an existence inspired in large part by life on the Atlantic coast. The shift from a purely extractive industry to one of planting and harvesting from well-tended beds required oystermen to keep in closer proximity to their intertidal and subtidal holdings. Growers built one- and two-story homes on pilings, clustering what were known as "station houses" near the most productive beds. As many as five or six workmen lived in a station at one time. Some station house residents spent weeks, months, and, in the case of oysterman Richard Murakami, entire years

in these outposts. "I was born there [in 1914]," Murakami told an interviewer from the Washington State Oral History Program. "We didn't move to land 'til I was about five years old." Living quarters occupied the top floor of a typical station house, with a kitchen, culling and shucking tables, plus a "box room," where the oysters were packed, filling the downstairs.

Although geographically isolated from life on land, the permanently occupied dwellings offered an extra advantage: as the industry grew, they became watch towers, guarding the shelled holdings against oyster pirates. One Bay Center oysterman claimed to have lost the equivalent of 300 sacks of oysters from one raid by these unscrupulous souls.

Indeed, securing one's oyster beds became a major focus during the early days of oyster culture, in Willapa Bay and throughout the Northwest. "The Indians who had used the natural lands for years as a food source could see the pinch coming," wrote Humphrey Nelson in his first-person adventure, *The Little Man and the Little Oyster*. "So they moved in, claimed squatters' rights, and were in the end allowed to purchase part of the acreage

Oyster growers relied on seasonal help. Many of these day laborers lived in tents (below)—suitable quarters during summer months. Oyster farmers' float houses (opposite) were anchored in the intertidal zone—as close to the action as one could possibly be.

they'd settled on. This angered some of the whites, who then bought land from the Indians or won it through gambling with them. Other whites married [Indians] to get their land, and in some cases there were shootings which got rid of someone in the way of a deal," the Shelton, Washington-born, Nelson noted.

Partly to clarify ownership of disputed tidelands, particularly in Puget Sound where many claims had yet to be staked, Washington's first state legislature passed what became known as the Callow Act of 1890. By official decree, oystermen were now entitled to purchase the lands they were working,

provided that no natural oyster beds existed on them. Five years later, legislators passed the Bush Act, extending the right to purchase waterfront acreage to anyone intent on oyster farming. Both acts had reversionary clauses: if lands were used for anything but oystering, the title would revert back to the state.

By establishing clear title to what had been tenuously held land, the Callow and Bush Acts helped oyster growers obtain working capital for their operations through bank loans. Much of this money was redirected into land acquisition. Under the Bush Act, individuals were entitled to buy up to 100 acres of oyster land at $1.25 per acre. By pooling their resources, Washington's intertidal entrepreneurs could amass considerable acreage, turning their already sizeable holdings into Texas-sized oyster estates.

In Puget Sound, oyster growers used their bank loans to finance construction of an elaborate system of terraces and dikes for Olympia oysters. In this regard, the Callow and Bush Acts stimulated cultivation practices throughout Washington's oyster empire. Production of Olympia oysters rose steadily over four decades, in large part because of these acts.

PLUNGERS AND POWER BOATS

Originating in Louisiana, bateaux were little more than broad skiffs, with washboards to keep their shelled contents from spilling over the sides.

Oyster boats also evolved and grew during this busy time, gradually resembling their more elegant counterparts from eastern ports. Instead of canoes and skiffs, harvesters became more reliant on small, graceful sailboats. There was good reason for this: wind-powered vessels could carry them greater distances to oyster beds throughout the bay. Up to 30 feet long and 10 feet wide, these versatile craft were known to both San Francisco

and Willapa Bay residents as plungers—a nickname possibly given, as one old-timer explained it, for this seaworthy vessel's abilities to plunge ahead in all kinds of weather.

"These early day oyster boats were half-decked, sloop rigged, with mainsail and jib, centerboard, square stern and a galley forward large enough to sleep two and contain a small stove for warmth and making coffee," recalled Emerson Watson, the son of one of Willapa's original oystermen.

On some plungers, the centerboard was nothing more than a flat plank of wood, permanently mounted on its keel for added stability when sailing into the wind. On others, this helpful feature could be pulled up, out of the water, allowing a crew to maneuver their craft over shallow reefs or shoals.

In the early 1870s, plunger owners formed the Shoalwater Bay Yacht Club at Oysterville, organizing a yearly regatta and a celebratory ball—the social event of the season. First to capture top honors at the sailing regatta was Edwin G. Loomis, owner of *Artemesia*, then the fastest sloop of her kind in the bay.

Not everyone could afford to participate in high-flown endeavors like racing. For many oystermen, simply staying afloat was a fulltime job. "When Dick Marion bought his sloop, she was past her best days and had a few leaks, but he drove her so hard she began to come apart," Emerson Watson remembered:

But Dick just couldn't take the time to haul her out and do a good repair job. Instead, he would caulk in a wad of oakum here and there in the worst places. It was always a case of pump or sink every few hours. Other boatmen working near him claimed he went to sleep at night with one leg on the floor, so when the water crawled up his pant leg he could get up and pump ship.

Unique to Washington's waters was the bateau, basically a barge with a pointed bow, low washboards enclosing an open, box-like center hold, and fringed with planking that served as a catwalk. A bateau's flat-bottomed hull was more buoyant and not as deep as other large vessels, making it better suited for carrying heavy loads in the shallows of the bay. These no-frills craft were seldom equipped with a sail; oyster tongers would propel them with long poles, cut and peeled from spruce saplings. Where the water was too deep to reach bottom, the bateau's operator could scull, driving the bateau forward with a stern-mounted oar.

More elaborate bateau designs featured a full deck, on which the oysters could be culled and cleaned before they were unloaded at station houses or shore facilities. They required no bailing—a real advantage over open-hulled bateaux and barges, especially in the perpetually rainy coastal Northwest.

Compared to their predecessors, plungers (above) were sleek and elegant—and plentiful, as this 1884 photograph from Bay Center, Washington (below), attests.

Motorized dredge boats (below and right) vastly increased the oyster harvester's efficiency. They remain the vessels of choice among Northwest growers.

As trade in eastern oysters expanded, oyster farmers turned to mechanization. By the turn of the century, motorized vessels started to appear alongside pole-powered and wind-driven ones. The owners of these craft often relied on their steam-powered engines for more than locomotion. They could now capitalize on the extra power to haul dredgefuls of oysters from the depths. Dumped in great heaps on deck, the dredge loads could be sorted and transferred to barrels or shoveled into floats, then brought to the oyster stations. Dredge technologies worked best with the larger, thick-shelled eastern oysters than with the smaller, more fragile Olympias.

THE CAUSE OF COLLAPSE

It's hard to imagine that such brisk business in farmed oysters could collapse. But that's exactly what happened, in the year 1919.

Why did things suddenly turn sour? Some say a virulent "red tide" swept through Willapa Bay, selectively wiping out eastern oysters while leaving the remnant native oysters unharmed. Others point to an oyster seed shortage in 1913, the result of unusually poor spawning conditions that afflicted the entire East Coast. Coupled with an exceptionally large harvest—around 19,000 gallons of oysters from Willapa in 1918—it's possible that the bay's cache of adult easterns had been picked clean.

Only after the oysters were gone was the ugly truth revealed: for some reason, quite possibly related to tides and water temperatures, the Northwest's stock of eastern oysters were not reproducing. Harvest rates and recruitment rates had been nowhere near commensurate.

Or *had* the eastern oysters all disappeared? Left unharvested, history suggests, eastern oysters could be capable of restocking their ranks. Periodically, a few holdouts are uncovered in Willapa Bay, most often at the mouth of the Naselle River, where in the distant past, a barge accidentally dumped its load of eastern oyster seed onto the seafloor. Salvage efforts were unsuccessful, and the resulting mat of adult oysters allegedly scattered their offspring throughout the bay. Only one self-sustaining

Workboat designs (below) have evolved in more recent times to accommodate the oyster grower's varied demands. Dredges in all shapes and sizes (overleaf and opposite) still ply the waters of Willapa and other Northwest bays.

population of eastern oysters has ever been discovered in the Northwest, at the mouth of the Nicomekl River in Boundary Bay, British Columbia. That population, albeit small, is still viable, with easterns coexisting with other oyster species on bars at the mouth of the river.

Some historians have proposed that the real cause of the industry's sudden collapse was economic, not biological. Well-staffed oyster stations and large steam-powered vessels were expensive to acquire, operate, and maintain. Routinely restocking oyster beds was also costly, especially considering the substantial losses en route and onsite. Having to wait four or five years while the oysters fattened and became ready for the market didn't exactly keep the cash flowing in.

For all of these reasons, it's conceivable that many principals in the eastern oyster trade became more dependent on moneylenders with each successive year on the tide flats. When a more cost-effective alternative presented itself, Northwest growers leapt at the chance to abandon the eastern oyster trade altogether. In so doing, they began a new chapter in the history of Northwest aquaculture—the Era of the Pacific Oyster.

THEY'RE ALL THE RAGE

When the native oysters grew short in supply, oyster lovers of the Pacific Northwest turned to the eastern variety, imported by rail from such places as New York and Baltimore. In many households, canned oysters became favored instead of fresh. A quick and delicious way to savor oysters from any location is scalloped. The recipe below is from a church cookbook published in Seattle, 1906.

SCALLOPED OYSTERS

Put an iron spider on the fire and get it very hot. Add a lump of butter the size of a walnut, then add a layer of cracker crumbs, then oysters, then crumbs, until the dish is full as can be handled. Add a cup of milk. Stir quickly, do not let brown. Add seasoning just before serving.

(From: *The Way We Ate: Pacific Northwest Cooking, 1843–1900* by Jacqueline B. Williams. Washington State University Press, Pullman, 1996)

AN EASTERN EXEMPLAR

On the East Coast, oyster consumption occurs under a stringent set of rules, depending on the location. As M. F. K. Fisher wrote in her 1941 book *Consider the Oyster*, "If a man cared, and knew all the rules, he would be frightened to go into a decent oyster bar and submit his knowledge to the cold eyes of the counterman and all the local addicts."

For the uninformed, she offered a glimpse of the appropriate. "Oysters are usually served on a plate of shaved ice, with small round white crackers in a bowl or vase. Quite often a commendable battery of bottled sauces such as Tabasco and horseradish accompanies the order, and in many restaurants a little cup of red sauce with a tomato base is put in the middle of the plate…."

For the enjoyment of any oysters on the half shell, she recommended the accompaniment of buttered brown bread and fresh juicy lemon.

Another way to enjoy them on the half shell is stuffed and lightly broiled; recipe follows.

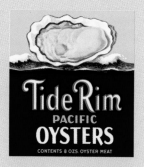

Scalloped Oysters (opposite). Oyster-inspired art may have reached a pinnacle on this classic can label (above) from a private collection.

STUFFED OYSTERS ON THE HALF SHELL

1 cup grated Parmesan cheese
1/2 cup finely diced green onions
1/2 cup finely diced red bell pepper
1/4 cup butter, softened
4 to 5 cloves garlic, minced
Juice of 1 lemon
2 tablespoons soy sauce
1 teaspoon sugar or honey
Pinch salt and pepper
12 medium oysters, shells well scrubbed

Combine the cheese, green onions, bell pepper, butter, garlic, lemon juice, soy sauce, sugar or honey, salt, and pepper in a medium bowl and stir to evenly blend. Preheat the broiler. Shuck the oysters, setting the cupped bottom shells in a shallow baking dish. Put an oyster in each shell and top with a generous tablespoon of the stuffing. Broil the oysters about 4 inches from the element until heated through and golden brown, about 8 minutes. Serve hot. Makes 4 servings.

(From: *The Wild Salmon Seafood Market's Guide to Northwest Oysters.* Wild Salmon Seafood Market at Fishermen's Terminal, Seattle, 2000.)

RIDING HIGH

If you're still hankering for a bit of the East Coast style, oysters from the Pacific Northwest can be just as glamorous when properly enrobed. Try this on for size— a recipe allegedly served to the elite passengers on the first train across Canada.

INAUGURATION STEW

³/₄ cup butter
1 cup sliced celery
2 carrots, shredded
6 green onions, chopped
1 medium leek, sliced
¹/₂ cup all-purpose flour
2 cups milk or half-and-half
Salt and pepper
1 pint oysters, drained
1 6¹/₂-ounce can minced clams
¹/₂ cup white wine or dry sherry

Heat ¹/₂ cup of the butter in a small saucepan over medium-low heat. Add the celery, carrots, green onions, and leek and cook gently for about 20 minutes. Heat the remaining ¹/₄ cup of the butter in a large saucepan over medium heat. Whisk in the flour and cook for a few minutes until the mixture begins to bubble, whisking constantly. Slowly whisk in the milk or half-and-half and continue cooking, whisking often, until the sauce thickens. Season to taste with salt and pepper, then stir in the vegetable mixture. In the saucepan that the vegetables were cooked in, combine the oysters, clams, and wine. Warm over low heat for about 10 minutes, stirring occasionally. Add the seafood mixture to the stew base and gently stir, then taste the stew for seasoning. Makes 4 servings.

(From: *Island Cookery: Seafood Specialties and All-time Favourites from Quadra Island, British Columbia.* Recipe from Hilda VanOrden, Quadra Island Child Care Society, 2000)

Whether purchased live (opposite), in cans (left), or in glass jars (above), oysters are welcome additions to any menu.

4. THE PACIFIC OYSTER PREMIERES

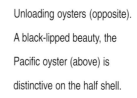

The question whether the Japanese oyster can be propagated in the United States on a large commercial scale has not been solved.

—Paul S. Galtsoff, U.S. Bureau of Fisheries, August 1932

In 1919, while Willapa's residents were worrying over the loss of livelihood due to the eastern oyster's decline, growers in northern Puget Sound were hard at work, readying their beds for another imported shellfish, the Pacific oyster (*Crassostrea gigas*) from Japan.

Hale and hearty, this species had been successfully cultured under similar oceanic and weather conditions for several centuries in Japan. Still there was reason to believe this foreign marvel might not thrive and multiply in North American seas.

To begin with, there was the difficulty of obtaining viable brood stock. Transporting live oysters from Japan could be an ordeal for both shellfish *and* shippers who eagerly awaited them. A typical ocean voyage from Japan to Washington took two and a half weeks—about the same as hauling oysters by freight train from the Atlantic or Gulf Coast states.

Throughout their long journey, the oysters had to be kept cool and moist. Few vessels in the early 1900s were equipped with refrigerated compartments. The only alternative was the windswept expanse of a ship's upper deck. As such, there was no guarantee that the oysterman's precious cargo would survive the long trip.

Unloading oysters (opposite). A black-lipped beauty, the Pacific oyster (above) is distinctive on the half shell.

What to do with the imported oysters once they arrived was another matter for concern. Would the Pacific oyster fall prey to the same mysterious ailment that had thwarted the Atlantic oyster's attempts at acclimation? Would it have special needs that might limit or preclude its transplantation? With the science of aquaculture still in its infancy, there were no definitive answers to these nagging questions.

STOCKS FROM OVERSEAS

Despite the formidable odds, two entrepreneurs stood ready to accept the challenge. J. Emi Tsukimoto and Joe Miyagi were residents of Olympia, Washington, yet had family ties that extended across the Pacific to the suppliers of Japan's superior oyster stocks. Both men possessed experience in the shellfish industry, having worked in the shucking house and shellfish beds of the J. J. Brenner Oyster Company.

Still, the pair faced several barriers to success—among them the accumulation of sufficient venture capital. To overcome this obstacle, Tsukimoto and Miyagi recruited partners from among Seattle's then-sizeable Japanese community. Six partners, some with ties to the seafood industry, signed aboard, electing Tsukimoto president of the newly formed Pearl Oyster Company.

One of the company's first acts was to purchase some prime waterfront real estate. Tsukimoto and Miyagi had staked out 600 acres of tideland on Samish Bay, south of Bellingham, Washington. It's said the two spent years investigating water and substrate conditions in several Puget Sound inlets before settling on this particular site for the Pacific oyster's point of introduction.

With its remaining money, Pearl Oyster Company bought 400 cases of Pacific oysters, grown in the Miyagi Prefecture and shipped in early April 1919 from the port of Yokohama in northern Japan. These fine specimens were loaded onto the deck of an American steamship, the *President McKinley*, covered with a protective layer of Japanese matting and given frequent showers of sea water to keep them fresh throughout the voyage.

PRESENTING THE PACIFIC OYSTER

CRASSOSTREA GIGAS

Roughly five times the size of its distant cousin, the eastern oyster, the Pacific oyster is the giant of Northwest shellfish beds. It is also one of the fastest-growing species, reaching sexual maturity in a year. In addition, it is better adapted than either of its distant relatives to enduring cold spells and other caprices of coastal weather.

For all these reasons, the Pacific is one of the most intensively cultivated oyster species in the world. Populations are now found in Australia, New Zealand, southwest Europe, Hawaii, and, of course, Japan. Introduced to North America in the early 1900s, it occurs from Southeast Alaska to northern Baja California and is cultured in all Pacific Northwest states, most intensively in Washington. In many estuarine areas where it is cultured, it is the dominant bivalve species.

The silver-gray meat of this oyster is sweet-tasting and rich, with a mild cucumber aftertaste. "It is best eaten uncooked on the half-shell or steamed, grilled, baked, poached, smoked or fried," says Braiden Rex-Johnson in the *Pike Place Public Market Seafood Cookbook*, adding that older, larger specimens are "best used in stews and pies."

Dock workers unload wooden cases of Pacific oyster seed from Japan, prior to World War II. As many as 50 gallons of meat could be obtained from the adult oysters reared from a single case of seed, according to E. N. Steele. His Rock Point Oyster Company imported a total of 12,802 cases of seed from 1922 to 1930.

The well-tended cargo—approximately 800 bushels of high-quality shellfish stock—arrived in Seattle 18 days later. Anxiously whisked past the U.S. Customs inspectors, the oysters were transferred to a small scow and carried with haste to Samish Bay.

When the scow landed, Pearl Oyster's people were in for a shock. Many of the larger oysters were dead on arrival. The rest were hastily transplanted to the company's beds, in the off chance of resuscitation. Any hopes of salvation were soon dashed, however, as these sole survivors slowly perished.

PHOENIX RISING

As it turned out, the experience was not a total loss for Pearl Oyster. Attached to the shells of the recently expired were hundreds of fingernail-sized spat—juvenile oysters that had apparently settled on their parents' calcareous crags in Japan. Like the mythological phoenix rising from the ashes, these youngsters would eventually grow to adulthood and become the first cash crop of Pacific oysters ever cultivated in the New World.

The discovery that spat could endure hardships the adults could not opened the door for the large-scale importation of Pacific oyster stocks. From then on, Northwest growers sought reliable suppliers of seed oysters with which they could easily rebuild their empty beds.

Seed oysters came in many shapes and sizes in the 1920s. The earliest shipments consisted primarily of spat-covered bamboo—the very material from which shellfish enclosures were constructed in northern Japan. Some seed producers also used lengths of tar-covered rope, dangled in the intertidal zone for the free-swimming larvae to fasten themselves onto. Others favored oyster shell, whole or broken into small bits, to facilitate shipping and easy dispersal on growing grounds.

At his Samish Bay facility, Pacific oysterman E. N. Steele experimented with all three kinds of seed, weighing the relative merits and drawbacks of each. "There was no question but that the seed caught on bamboo and the brush was very heavy in numbers, and a box of that type of seed contained many more oysters

Today, E. N. Steele's son Dick (below) presides over the Rock Point Oyster Company. He takes pleasure in the sight of expansive oyster beds, including this one (opposite), photographed by family friend Dr. Trevor Kincaid.

than the type caught on shell," he wrote in *The Immigrant Oyster*, a comprehensive overview of the Pacific oyster's earliest days in the Northwest.

Eventually Steele and his contemporaries found oyster shell more to their liking. Because of its heft and flat shape, this form of seed was more prone to stay in place, even along the wave-battered shoreline of northern Hood Canal, the present site of the Steele family's Rock Point Oyster Company.

THE OYSTERS' NEW OWNER

In the spring of 1921, Steele paid a visit to Pearl Oyster's property. Here he met Tsukimoto, Miyagi, and the bivalve that would eventually claim the lion's share of aquacultural activity in the Northwest.

"The sun was just coming up over the mountain tops," Steele later recalled. "Its light glittered over the oysters. They stood up in large clusters and the new growth, the lip of the oysters, transparent in the sunlight, appeared to be an inch long. I stood and looked in amazement."

After two years in the plankton-rich waters of northern Puget Sound, Washington's Japanese transplants had grown from near-microscopic spat to adult specimens with shells over six inches in length. By Steele's calculation, it would take only 120 of these mega-mollusks to yield a gallon of shucked meat— a twenty-fifth of the Olympia oysters required to produce the same quantity for the Rock Point Oyster Company.

While a sophomore at the University of Washington in 1897, Trevor Kincaid (opposite, left and right) was offered his first teaching job. "Scientific men in this state were just about zero then," he noted with characteristic modesty. He later joined the UW's faculty as a professor of zoology.

Encouraged by such profitable prospects, Samish Bay's resident shellfish expert was determined to start rearing Pacific oysters posthaste. The following spring, he again visited Miyagi and Tsukimoto, intent on purchasing Pearl Oyster Company's beds. It took a year of negotiation, but in 1923 the oyster growers agreed on a fair price, and ownership of all 600 acres was passed to Steele and his partner, J. C. Barnes of Olympia.

Steele was indirectly assisted in his acquisition efforts by the passage of Washington's Anti-Alien Land Act of 1921. Enacted amidst a climate of anti-Japanese sentiment, this piece of legislation prohibited anyone but lawfully registered U.S. citizens from owning properties within the state. It extended this prohibition to every interest in land, and any "right to control, possession, use, enjoyment, rents, issues, or profits thereof." Under the terms of the act, land owned by aliens could be confiscated by the state and later sold at auction.

Faced with an uncertain future, Pearl Oyster's Japanese owners were "discouraged to the point where they wanted to dispose of their interest in the land and sell the oysters planted thereon," according to Steele.

Within a month of the company's sale, J. Emi Tsukimoto boarded a freighter on Seattle's waterfront, bound for Japan. From across the ocean he continued to shape the Northwest's shellfish industry, supplying Steele and others with reliable sources of Pacific oyster seed. Joe Miyagi also left for Japan, where he assisted shellfish growers in the prefecture for which he was named.

THE SCHOLAR AND THE SCHEMER

Equally instrumental in the establishment of Pacific oysters in the Northwest was Professor Trevor Kincaid, a professor of zoology at the University of Washington. While his early passion was the study of insects, Kincaid became fascinated with plankton and oyster culture in 1911. In the early 1920s, he operated the Washington State Department of Fisheries oyster laboratory in Bay Center (which later moved to nearby Nahcotta) on Willapa Bay and continued his research. Later, the

hard-working scientist was listed in *Who's Who* and in 1938 received the University of Washington's highest honor as an *alumnus summa laude dignatus*. In 1979, the state's renovated research facility in Brinnon was dedicated to the scholar—the Trevor Kincaid Shellfish Laboratory at Point Whitney.

During his years at the Bay Center lab, Kincaid "practically established the Japanese oyster industry at Willapa Harbor," according to Seattle historian Melville Hatch. E. N. Steele benefited from the good doctor's

expertise, as did Gerard Mogan, a venture capitalist with an eye on the oyster industry. At Kincaid's suggestion, Mogan started exploring the convoluted coast of Willapa Bay during the late 1920s. After an initial planting of Pacific oyster seed proved promising, Mogan began buying up land, some of it for as little as 38 cents an acre. When asked about his plans for developing his shoreline holdings, the routinely tight-lipped Mogan replied he was planning to cultivate clams—a response "which made the wiseacres smile," according to Kincaid.

Slowly but surely, Mogan gained ownership of about 7,000 acres of oyster-friendly tideland. He formed a corporation, the Baypoint Oyster Farms and, with $100,000 in capital, ordered 1,700 cases

These three land sharks (opposite) were featured in a promotional piece from 1931, printed by the Willapa Development Company of Seattle. "There is perhaps no acre of land on earth more productive than a Willapa Bay oyster bed," the booklet boasted. "Health and income await the enterprising oyster farmer."

of seed from Tsukimoto. Buoyed by Mogan's optimism and the results of his previous test planting of Pacifics, three other shellfish growers joined in, ordering an additional 1,280 cases of seed.

The next year, Mogan founded a second corporation, the Willapa Oyster Farms, ordering 2,000 cases of seed for each of his two ventures. Securing massive quantities of seed was no mean feat, even for a moneyed land baron like Mogan. When the steamship company that carried the seed insisted on landing in Seattle, a distance of 100 miles from the ocean coast, Mogan commandeered a group of unused railroad cars, hurriedly loaded them with seed cases, and hauled them to Aberdeen, where a fleet of trucks stood waiting to transport the live cargo to dispersal sites at Toke Point.

By now, the number of local growers importing seed had increased to 15. "The boom was on," proclaimed Kincaid. "A number of faulty promotions took place and land was planted that was unsuitable for the purpose, resulting in considerable losses."

Many of those faulty promotions were traced to a Seattle real estate company, which in the 1930s began

offering long, narrow slivers of Mogan's oyster-growing properties to buyers with get-rich-quick fantasies. Some of those shoreline strips, hindsight has it, were worthless. The oyster beds on these parcels were completely submerged (hence extremely difficult to plant, tend, or harvest from) at all but the most extreme low tides. The same ploy was used to bilk individuals into acquiring worthless properties along Padilla Bay and other northern Puget Sound locales.

"A snappy sales job explained the success of those promotions," according to Nancy Lloyd, author of the self-published *Willapa Bay & The Oysters*. "In the early '30s, the Japanese sold seed for $3 a case," she related. "That case could produce 150 gallons of mature oysters. Each acre of tideland would take up to 20 cases of seed, and so could in theory produce 3,000 gallons of meat which sold for $.50 to $1.00 per gallon. So if tideland cost $150 an acre, the seed cost $60, and the labor to spread the seed over that acre was between $5 and $10, the owner's costs were around $220. The oysters from that acre sold for $1,500 to $3,000, yielding a staggering profit."

PROLIFIC PACIFICS

Oysters took to the skies (opposite) when the Brenners expanded their sales base in the 1920s. The pilot of this Rhodes Brothers biplane is Leon Titus, but nobody—not even the Brenners—knows who the two salesmen are.

While some wannabe oyster farmers lost their shirts, other, more experienced growers cashed in on the Pacific's popularity. Thanks in large part to Willapa Bay's contribution to an already booming market for Pacifics, the state's production of oyster meat nearly quintupled—from 6,500 gallons in 1929 to 31,000 gallons in 1931. Output skyrocketed over the next ten years, reaching a record 1,131,100 gallons in 1941. Smaller peaks in production occurred in British Columbia, Oregon, and northern California.

Not everyone in the Northwest was as appreciative of the new oyster species as the growers would've liked. Steele discovered that some consumers were reluctant to try something new. As he made the rounds of Seattle-area restaurants and fish markets, he found that each owner had initial objections and, as he put it, "had to be shown that their business would be increased by making the change" from imported easterns to locally grown Pacific oysters. Some buyers felt the Pacific oyster's characteristically dark-rimmed flesh made it appear unappetizing. Steele overcame this prejudice with a snappy advertising campaign. "Look for the oysters with the velvet rim," his printed advertisements proclaimed. "It assures you that it is grown in the pure waters of Puget Sound."

Others were unaccustomed to the new oyster's large size—even in its native country, chopstick-wielding Japanese found the Pacific oyster an ungainly foodstuff, preferring instead to sup on smaller species and subspecies. Steele won over these skeptics with cooking demonstrations, staged by his brother and sister-in-law with a three-burner electric hot plate. Shoppers were offered fried oysters and shown how to make what Steele called a cracker sandwich. "Many of those who liked the sample would purchase a can of oysters, and were assured that this market would keep a supply for future use," he wrote. Further sales assistance came from the Home Economics Department at the University of Washington, which coproduced a folder of sample recipes featuring the savory Pacific oyster.

Steele's persuasive presentations and promotional materials worked remarkably well. In one day, workers at the Portland Fish Market sold $80 worth of Pacific oysters, at 35 cents for a half-pint and 65 cents for a pint. Buoyed with optimism, Steele bought a small Dodge truck, fitted it with sleeping quarters for his sales staff, and packed it with advertising materials and painted oyster shells. This oysters-on-wheels operation spread the word about Pacific oysters as far south as San Bernardino, California, and as far east as Salt Lake City.

"There was hardly a market of any size along the coast that we had not called upon," Steele reminisced. "The orders were very small in comparison with present-day orders. Yet they were sufficient to dispose of our crops as they increased from year to year."

Other oyster growers followed, literally, in Steele's salesmen's footsteps. With massive quantities of Pacific oysters to sell, Willapa's growers soon dominated the market, unintentionally driving down oyster prices with their surpluses. Although smaller-scale operations such as Steele's suffered, there was enough business in oysters for everyone to benefit to a degree. No longer viewed

Three of Willapa Bay's future empire builders (left to right)—Dobby, Jack, and Lee Wiegardt—wade with their cousin, Marian Craxberger. After World War II, seed buyers and seed inspectors from the Pacific Coast Oyster Growers Association (opposite) haunted several Japanese ports, occasionally accompanied by family members.

with suspicion, the immigrant oyster was now regarded as a "naturalized" citizen of Northwest shores, one with a solid reputation for conferring wealth on its cultivators.

Assured of a steady supply of seed from Japan, there was little reason to believe that stocks of

Pacific oysters would ever decline. Who could predict that events in a remote Pacific harbor with an ironically appropriate name—Pearl Harbor—would put a sudden end to the industry's rapid rise and send oystermen scurrying for new sources of seed?

OYSTER FARMERS UNITE!

While the work may have been dirty, the dollars it brought were quite clean. Charles Fitzpatrick of Ocean Park, Washington, took this photograph (opposite) of Willapa Bay oyster farmers in 1935. Many of Fitzpatrick's images were printed as postcards glorifying the good but grimy life of the oysterman.

By 1929, Washington state's oyster production outweighed consumer demand for the first time in the history of the West Coast industry. Prior to this point, there had been no need for mutually accepted standards for marketing or sales. With the increasingly competitive climate in which most oystermen operated, it was soon obvious that some form of self-regulation was required.

In the spring of 1930, Myron T. Heuston of Willapa Bay's Long Island Oyster Company called together a few interested growers for a meeting in South Bend. This gathering proved the catalyst for a larger meeting in August of the same year, when the Pacific Coast Shellfish Growers Association officially came into being. In attendance were many notable oystermen whose names remain synonymous with the oyster business today—E. N. Steele, Earl Brenner, Frank Wiegardt, and Trevor Kincaid.

Originally dubbed the North Pacific Oyster Growers Association, this group has since gone through two name changes: first as the Pacific Coast Oyster Growers Association in 1934, then the Pacific Coast Shellfish Growers Association (a name reflective of the organization's recently expanded role) in 1999.

In those early days, finding markets for the prolific Pacific oyster and stabilizing prices were among two of the most important missions of the association. Recognizing that the tasks at hand would require a professional, the association had hired its first executive secretary, Fitzherbert Leather, who had prior experience with an advertising agency in Seattle. Charley Pollock succeeded Leather in 1934, and the association took on a new role as the West Coast's chief buyer and distributor of Japanese oyster seed.

In the late 1940s, the group again broadened its scope to include anti-pollution activities. Because of the oyster growers' dependence on the environment, work in this arena remains a critical mission of the PCSGA. The single most important task facing the association is the development of a set of uniform operating codes for the shellfish industry, from Alaska to California. These codes are being designed to ensure that shellfish farming operations use the best possible management techniques to protect the marine environment in which their oysters and other cultured bivalves grow.

Marketing issues remain a focus of the PCSGA. From its headquarters in Olympia, its members sponsor special events that tout the culinary and environmental benefits of shellfish and help growers capitalize on the sales capacity of the Internet—an inconceivable development to marketers in the PCSGA's formative years.

THE WAY WE WERE

When K. Honda, of Sendai, Japan, visited Willapa Harbor back in 1953, his goal was to observe the scope and progress of an industry started by a countryman of his 38 years before—that is, the importation of Japanese oyster seed to growers in the U.S. During his visit, members of the Pacific Coast Oyster Growers Association told him about their efforts to promote three leading oyster dishes: butter fry, bacon wrapped, and wine broiled. When asked how oysters were eaten in Japan, he replied, "The most popular way is fried. My people also like raw oysters in vinegar, and oysters in soybean mash, sukiyaki style. I don't think you can visualize what that last one is like…." Rather than imagining this last one, try these variations on the above-mentioned West Coast favorites instead.

OYSTERS BAKED WITH GINGER CRANBERRY PORT SAUCE

½ cup butter, softened
2 tablespoons minced fresh ginger
2 cups whole cranberries
½ cup port
Juice of ½ lemon
2 tablespoons brown sugar
¼ teaspoon raspberry vinegar
24 extra small Pacific oysters, shells well scrubbed
Rock salt
Chopped toasted walnuts, for garnish

Mix the butter with the ginger until well blended, then set aside. Combine the cranberries, port, lemon juice, brown sugar, and raspberry vinegar in a small saucepan and cook over high heat, stirring often, until the mixture reduces by half. Purée the cranberry mixture in a food processor, then press it through a fine sieve. Shuck the oysters, saving the cupped bottom shells. Lay rock salt on an ovenproof platter and nestle the reserved shells in the salt to stabilize them. Put about ¼ teaspoon of the ginger butter in each shell and set an oyster on top. Spoon about 1 tablespoon of the cranberry port sauce over each oyster. Bake at 450°F for no more than 8 to 10 minutes. Garnish with toasted walnuts. Makes 4 servings.

(From: *The New Ark Cookbook: Fresh and Simple Cuisine from the Pacific Northwest* by Nanci Main and Jimella Lucas. Chronicle Books, San Francisco, California, 1990)

Oysters Baked with Ginger Cranberry Port Sauce (opposite). Two well-known family names—Wiegardt and Wilson—adorn these classy labels (opposite, below) from the halcyon days of Willapa Bay's shellfish canneries.

Several unique oyster recipes have been developed, including this one by Michael Flynn, executive chef with the Alyeska Prince Hotel in Southeast Alaska. The oysters are slathered with Pesto and presented on a stately bed of greens, topped with Vinaigrette. It doesn't get much better than this.

PESTO ROASTED OYSTERS

16 medium or large Pacific oysters in the shell
2 ripe tomatoes, quartered and seeded
2 ounces mixed baby greens (mesclun)

PESTO:

Leaves from 2 bunches fresh basil, picked from the stems
    (about 2 to 3 cups loosely packed) and blanched
2 tablespoons finely chopped garlic
2 tablespoons grated Parmesan cheese
2 tablespoons toasted pine nuts
1/2 cup olive oil, or more to achieve desired consistency
Salt and freshly ground black pepper to taste

VINAIGRETTE:

1 tablespoon Dijon-style mustard
1/4 cup good-quality red or balsamic vinegar
1/2 cup olive oil
1 tablespoon chopped fresh mixed herbs

To make the Pesto, place the blanched basil and garlic in a food processor. Pulse until the basil is coarsely chopped. Add the Parmesan cheese and pine nuts. With the motor running, add the oil slowly in a steady stream until the mixture is emulsified and reaches a soft paste consistency. Add salt and pepper to taste.

To make the Vinaigrette, place the mustard, vinegar, oil, and herbs in a jar and shake vigorously until mixed.

Preheat the broiler.

Wash the oysters well under cold water to remove any dirt or grit. Open them with a shucking knife and loosen the meat from the shell. Cut the tomato quarters into halves diagonally. Place a piece of tomato in the bottom of each shell, with an oyster on top. Top each oyster with 1 teaspoon of the Pesto. Place under the broiler for 6 to 10 minutes.

Divide the baby greens among 4 salad plates. Drizzle some of the Vinaigrette over and around the greens.

Place 4 oysters, evenly spaced, atop the greens on each plate. Serve immediately. Makes 4 servings.

(From: *The Alaska Heritage Seafood Cookbook* by Ann Chandonnet. Alaska Northwest Books, Portland, Oregon, 1995)

OYSTERS WRAPPED IN BACON

6 slices pepper bacon, cut in half crosswise
12 medium shucked oysters
Juice of ½ lime
Lime wedges and parsley sprigs, for garnish

Lay out the 12 pieces of bacon on a rimmed baking sheet and broil until half done but still limp. Wrap each oyster with one piece of the bacon and pierce with a toothpick to hold it in place. Bake at 350°F until the bacon is crispy and the oysters are cooked through, about 10 minutes. Sprinkle with the lime juice and garnish with the lime wedges and parsley. Makes 4 to 6 servings.

(From: Chef Eric Jenkins, Duncan Law Seafood Consumer Center, Astoria, Oregon, 2000)

PANÉED OYSTERS

1½ cups Italian seasoned bread crumbs
1 cup all-purpose flour
1 teaspoon finely ground black pepper
½ teaspoon salt
12 shucked oysters, drained
½ cup olive oil
1 tablespoon grated Romano cheese

Mix the bread crumbs, flour, pepper, and salt together in a large bowl. Dredge the oysters in the crumb mixture. Heat the olive oil in a large skillet over high heat. Fry the oysters in 2 batches for 1¼ minutes on the first side and 45 seconds on the second side. Transfer the oysters to a plate and sprinkle with the Romano cheese. Makes 4 servings.

(From: *Oysters* by John DeMers and Andrew Jaeger. Celestial Arts Press, Berkeley, California, 1999)

Lovingly prepared by Northwest packers, smoked oysters (below) were in high demand throughout the 1950s and 1960s. Today these delicacies are mainly imported from Korea and Taiwan.

5. OYSTERS IN WAR AND PEACE

Oystermen of Olympia predict that they will have difficulty in finding white men to work the oyster beds and canneries when the Japanese are evacuated.

—Arthur L. Schoeni, United Press writer, April 9, 1942

We were opening oysters for Eagle Rock that Sunday morning," recalled Jeff Murakami of South Bend, Washington. "Somebody came in and told us that Japan had bombed us at Pearl Harbor. We all stopped our work. [We] were so shocked."

For Murakami and other oystermen of Japanese ancestry, the war, however distant, would have immediate, damaging effects. Within six months of the Japanese attack at Pearl Harbor on December 7, 1941, the Murakami family would be whisked off to an internment camp, leaving their second-generation oyster farm to tend itself.

Jeff's brother, Itsuyuki "Ira" Murakami, had worked in the oyster industry since 1912, when he applied for a job at the Johnson McGowan Oyster Company on Willapa Bay. Ira had been among the first to seed the bay with imported oyster seed, purchased through family contacts in his homeland. His son Richard worked alongside his father at Eagle Rock Cannery and elsewhere in the industry. The family also farmed a cranberry bog, a few miles inland from their oyster beds.

Four years later, when World War II ended and the Murakamis returned to their

Relaxing at the end of a workday (opposite). Algae-encrusted oyster shell (below), the mainstay of longline culture.

family farm, they found their oyster beds stripped of everything even remotely edible. The cranberries, too, had been harvested without permission, but at least these could replenish themselves in a few seasons. Even with the best of weather and the most tender care, it would take several years for the oysters to repopulate their beds.

No longer able to support themselves on their holdings, the Murakamis sold their waterfront property to Coast Oyster Company—then, as now, one of Washington's largest oyster farming operations. As part of the deal, Coast Oyster offered Richard a job in its cannery. He excelled, moving up from bed supervisor to master mechanic, and finally to production manager—a position he retained until retirement in the late 1970s.

Ira Murakami didn't fare well in the postwar world. He died in 1952, "broken-hearted and depressed," in the words of his family, "because of the loss of his and his wife's life work."

Puget Sound oysterman Jerry Yamashita also suffered the consequences of war with Japan. His budding career as an oysterman was abruptly interrupted at age 19, when his family was moved to an internment camp.

Jerry recalls being watched with suspicion during the weeks preceding his family's internment. "For his oyster seed business, my father kept nautical charts with information on depths and currents all along the West Coast. That alone made us appear suspect—as if we would be using this information to help guide the enemy to our shores," he explains.

Hoping to forestall their inevitable arrest, the Yamashitas drove 90 miles from their oyster farm on

Samish Bay to Seattle, where Jerry's father kept an office at one of the city's waterfront piers. Here, the family tried to destroy the potentially damaging evidence before it could fall into the wrong hands.

"We couldn't burn the charts without attracting all sorts of attention," says Yamashita. "So in the end we just left a note for the pier's owner, asking if he'd take the office furniture and other things in lieu of the last month's rent. Then we drove home."

Yamashita later learned that by venturing more than five miles from their residence, his family had already broken the law. "Had we been caught, we would have been in big trouble," he recalls.

Released from the internment camp in 1945, the 23-year-old Yamashita returned to oyster farming. He bought tidal property on Hood Canal, dug a well, and scraped together materials to build a small shack where he both lived and worked. With these humble beginnings, the Western Oyster Company was born. Yamashita continues to farm oysters in southern Puget Sound, nearly six decades after the war.

"Some Japanese-American oystermen were fearful about returning to Washington state," Richard Murakami later told readers of the *Chinook Observer* newspaper in Long Beach. "They thought the best thing was to stay away until things kind of cooled down. I told them, 'If you do that, you'll never get back. You better fight it out and get established and if you don't want to do it, I'll go ahead and do it.' "

World War II affected every oyster farmer, not only those of Japanese descent. No one in the industry, young or old, could escape the sacrifices and hardship of those uncertain times. It was difficult for most business owners to obtain the necessary raw materials—wood for packing crates, tin and glass for cans and jars, fuel to power their trucks and oyster boats. Experienced workers were also in short supply.

A number of Northwest growers declined to seek agricultural deferments to the draft. Answering the call to defend their nation, they voluntarily left their family oyster beds in the hands of women, children, and senior citizens. To the credit of these hastily recruited helpers, most oyster beds remained productive throughout the war years.

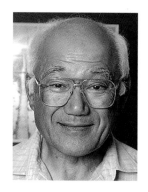

American-born Richard Murakami (opposite) and Jerry Yamashita (above) suffered during the World War II years. Despite enormous setbacks, they remained active in the oyster industry and are highly respected by their peers.

AN UNEXPECTED BOUNTY

Conditions were kind to those left tending the beds. Fortunately the years preceding Pearl Harbor had been exceptionally mild and nurturing for the transplanted Pacific oyster stocks. In the mid-1930s the Pacific coast had been bathed in unusually warm seas, the hallmark of El Niño, an ocean current that flows northward from the tropics every three to seven years. Often accompanying El Niño currents are localized blooms of phytoplankton, the oyster's food. The combination of favorable conditions and better nutrition caused the Pacific oyster populations to explode.

Veteran oystermen reminisce about the summer of 1936, when their bay was awash with oyster larvae from El Niño-influenced spawning. Oyster spat clung to boulders, breakwaters, docks and pilings, rusted anchors, even the bottoms of bateaux and work boats. Some old-timers claim the bay suffered from too much of a good thing—that the unchecked appetites of the infant Pacific oysters actually stripped Willapa Bay of its food and dissolved mineral resources.

"There was no place to run, no place where the water would not be filtered and refiltered a thousand times over by the fantastic numbers of hungry little mouths," wrote Al Qualmann in *Blood on the Half Shell*, his personal history. The oysters haven't grown as quickly or as big since that particular feast, many farmers maintain.

Several of Willapa's growers had been devastated by the Great Depression, which had severely strained the nation's pocketbooks, keeping shoppers away from seafood markets throughout the U.S. But those who survived optimistically continued to plant their beds with oyster seed from Japan. E. N. Steele calculated that at the time of Pearl Harbor, over 1.5 million gallons of Willapa oysters were waiting to be harvested and consumed. For the first time, growers had now amassed enough stock for their shellfish to be self-sustaining—an important benchmark in the history of Northwest aquaculture.

A surplus of oysters was not so great for the people who cultivated and sold them. The massive quantities of fresh oysters and shucked meats further depressed an already subdued marketplace, forcing growers to lower their prices and look farther afield for sales. Several savvy individuals turned to canning—a procedure that had already proved its worth in the salmon, sardine, tuna, abalone, and squid fisheries. Canning could extend the shelf life of an oyster by months, even years. Packed tightly, several dozen tins to a crate, canned oysters could be sent by rail or flown by airplanes to every corner of the country—even to other oyster-growing areas on the Atlantic and Gulf coasts.

"Something for which America has been waiting," proclaimed the promotional material for the Padilla Point Oyster Company of Everett, Washington. "At last a perfect canning oyster has been developed, unlike any known before…in tenderness and flavor…in shape and size it surpasses the former, fancy Baltimore packs."

Among the first to capitalize on canning? None other than Gerard Mogan, who in 1932 contracted with a South Bend–based packing company for a test run of 1,000 cases of cans. When his experiment yielded satisfactory results, Mogan built his own makeshift cannery, shipping steamed, hermetically sealed Pacific

oysters in 6-, 8-, and 12-ounce tins with colorful Willapoint, Bay Point, and Willapa Oyster Farms labels.

"Mogan was primarily a promoter rather than a businessman, and spent money very lavishly in promoting the sale of stock and in opening up the market," conceded Trevor Kincaid in *The Ecology of Willapa Bay, Washington, in Relation to the Oyster Industry*. South Bend historian Doug Allen concurs with Kincaid's assessment, pointing to a 1934 letter from Mogan's secretary-treasurer I. L. Steinhaus apologizing to stockholders for the lack of dividends, despite what had been a very satisfactory year. However remorseful, Steinhaus couldn't end his letter without an advertising pitch, reminding his readers that no other canned oysters could compare to Willapoint's.

Modern technologies have greatly increased the yield from each acre of oyster-growing tideland. Savvy oyster growers can keep shellfish processors busy throughout the year.

CANNERY DAYS

Early oyster canneries were big, busy, and oftentimes rudimentary places. Wholly devoted to mass production, they offered few concessions to worker comfort or workplace aesthetics. Money for new construction was tight during the Depression, so cannery owners were forced to economize, sometimes to the extreme. Wood for the Northern Oyster Company's plant (built in 1933 on the site of the present-day Oysterville Sea Farms) was salvaged from the wreck of the S.S. *Iowa*, a lumber ship that ran aground at Peacock Spit. The cannery's underpinnings came from the old Ellsworth railway bridge and its boiler from an abandoned "logging donkey"—a steam-powered engine for harvesting timber. The total cost of constructing Northern Oyster's jury-rigged facility has been estimated at about $3,300.

Canning oysters in the 1930s and early 1940s was "kind of a crude process," according to Dobby Wiegardt, grandson of one of the industry's founders, Heinrich Julius Wiegardt. Heinrich's sons, Fred and

John, built the Wiegardt Brothers cannery in Nahcotta, Washington. When not canning oysters, their employees kept busy, processing whatever the Wiegardts sent their way, whether beef or blackberries, Dungeness crab, razor clams, or salmon roe.

Beneath a cannery's galvanized tin roof, day laborers toiled around the clock, opening trays of oysters and cramming the fresh or lightly cooked meats into various-sized containers. "We would put maybe about two bushels of oysters on a tray and then pile another tray on top of that until we had six trays on a truck and then we would cook them in a retort, I think [for] 20 minutes or so," Dobby explained to one interviewer.

The short time in the steaming retort made the oyster shells gape, making it easier for the openers to do their jobs. A large cannery might employ as many as 20 openers per shift, paying them wages based on the volume of oysters they could make ready for canning. With little more than a sharp knife and cloth gloves, a skilled opener could process about 30 gallons during an eight-hour shift. At eight pounds of oysters in a gallon,

that pencils out to about 240 pounds in a day—or about 1,200 pounds of the soft, grayish meats per week. Some canneries operated three shifts of openers, and, when the demand called for it, kept the shifts busy seven days a week. Thus, peak output sometimes approached 75,000 pounds of canned oysters per week. Padilla Point, by its own assessment "the largest salmon cannery in the world...as well the largest oyster

Women found decent pay at Northwest oyster canneries (opposite) and dominated the workforce at canneries during World War II (below).

Punching holes in empty oyster shells and stringing the shells to make cultch were jobs for even the youngest worker on an oyster farm.

"I like the work," June Iverson told a reporter for *The Seattle Times.*

"Once you get used to the job, you can think of other things and work really fast, too."

During the war, canning was curtailed because of the lack of materials. But business resumed in 1946, when there were reportedly 89,050 cases of oysters canned in Washington. In 1941, the last canning year before the war, there were 178,445 cases of oysters canned in Washington.

Like Upton Sinclair's description of the hog butchery, where "they use everything except the squeal," cannery owners found ways of wringing profit from every ounce of the oyster. Calcium-laden oyster shells were ground into powder and sold as an ingredient in cement mixes, soil amendments, and poultry feed. Any shells left unsold were bagged, bundled, or strung on long lines, transforming the shucker's refuse into valuable cultch media. The word "cultch," by some accounts, is the abbreviated term for culture medium. Others claim the word crept into our language via French aquaculturists and their term,

cannery," had the capacity to assemble 2,000 cases of canned oysters daily.

In 1947, Haines Oyster Company employed nine women openers, who listened to country music on the radio while they shucked gallons of oysters, either for quick freeze in Seattle or the cannery in Willapa Bay. The women earned 55 cents per gallon, considered good pay at the time.

couche, or "couch." Regardless of where the term originated, it basically means the same thing—material placed on the oyster grounds, upon which future generations of oysters can attach themselves and grow. Oyster growers have learned to bundle the empty oyster shells in mesh bags or to string them on wires. By suspending the bags and strings of cultch from rafts or lacing them between poles in suitable locales, they can collect sufficient seed stock to replant their oyster beds. Instead of oyster shell, some intertidal farmers use cement-coated wooden lath or egg crates, plastic pipes, and metal screening to gather Olympia oyster seed.

The abundance of highly nutritious oysters and the technology to efficiently process and deliver them far afield did not go unnoticed by the War Department. In October 1943, an Army representative approached Arnold Waring of the Haines Oyster Company, offering to buy all the oysters that he and other Willapa Bay growers could provide, frozen and delivered to Seattle. The Army would pay from $3.25 to $3.75 per gallon, depending on the grade—that is, the size—of the shellfish supplied.

Waring urged his fellow oystermen to devote at least 60 percent of their yearly output to feeding the troops. Recognizing an opportunity to assist in the war effort while turning a tidy profit, E. N. Steele and other members of the Pacific Coast Oyster Growers Association unanimously accepted the government's terms. To be of further service, they agreed to hold down their prices on all future sales and to convince secondary wholesalers and retailers to do the same.

In the years that followed, PCOGA members also developed a set of standards for the industry that would guarantee all oysters sold would be of consistent, high quality. From then on, cans would be clearly labeled so that consumers could tell at a glance what kind of oyster—Olympia, eastern, or Pacific—was being sold and how many were in a container.

Patriotism coupled with government contracts inspired Washington's oyster farmers to work overtime. From 1943 to 1946, production levels for Willapa Bay nearly doubled, attaining a historic peak of about 13.2 million pounds of oyster meats. One operation alone, the Wiegardt Oyster Company, provided the military

Cement-covered egg crates were a preferred cultch medium for capturing Olympia oyster spat (overleaf). Farmers would lay down the crates in the diked tidelands of Puget Sound and let Mother Nature take her course.

with about 100,000 gallons of succulent Pacifics, packed 36 shucked oysters to the six-pound container. In return, the Army decorated the company's president, Fred Wiegardt, with its Award for Excellence.

The large-scale technologies devised before and after World War II helped to stabilize the oyster industry. Because they could now process and store enormous quantities of oyster meats, growers were less strongly affected by the seasonal cycles and the ups and downs inherent in any natural resource-based operation. Empowered by this degree of certainty, they were free to experiment with new processing techniques and products. It was during this brief period of calm between storms that growers introduced the so-called "cocktail" oyster. The size of a 25-cent piece, this tasty tidbit was slowly smoked over a fire of crabapple wood chips and packed in cottonseed oil—perfect for piercing with a party pick. Unfortunately, the era of these locally produced domestic delicacies was killed in the 1950s by competition from canneries in Japan and Korea, whose exports undercut local processors' prices.

POST-WW II TRIALS AND TRIUMPHS

At the close of the war, soldiers returned to their home towns of the Pacific Northwest, eager to resume the activity they knew best: raising oysters. A cursory inspection of their oyster beds, however, told them that several years of hard labor now lay ahead. The marine climate had again shifted, away from the warming El Niño to a cooler, La Niña current regime.

For the previous two years, lower water temperatures had depressed the natural spawning and setting activities in Willapa and other Northwest bays. Simultaneously, the drive to supply the canneries with what had been perceived as a bumper crop of oysters had invariably depleted even the most productive shellfish growing areas. Without large quantities of imported oyster seed to scatter around, it was doubtful that Northwest oyster beds could rebuild themselves in due time.

Unfortunately, Japanese seed suppliers were in just as bad, if not worse, shape, business-wise. In 1945, when U.S. officials conducted a tour of Japanese aquaculture stations, they returned with horror stories of the war-ravaged seed oyster industry in Hiroshima and Miyagi prefectures. Later that year, General Douglas MacArthur asked the Japanese government to export 80,000 boxes of oyster seed to the U.S. The head of the occupation forces was told what no Northwest growers wanted to hear: that it would take considerable time and money to rebuild much-neglected and seriously understaffed coastal facilities before any foreign shipments could be made.

Within months of MacArthur's request, the Japanese had converted a sea-salt processing plant into the Kumamoto Prefecture Oyster Seed Export Training Center. The next year, according to Japanese shellfish biologist Fusao Ota, they shipped the first batch of seed in nearly six years—30 boxes of juvenile Kumamoto oysters (*Crassostrea sikamea*), slated for test plantings in Puget Sound beds.

Some of the seedlings thrived, while others perished in their new environs. The survivors reached Olympia-like proportions in about eight months, attaining a slightly larger size in another one to two years. Marketed as the "Western Gem," the Kumamoto found ready

ED GRUBLE, THE CZAR OF OYSTER STEW

Even in retirement, Ed Gruble keeps tabs on the oyster industry from his West Seattle, Washington, home.

New England has its clam chowder, but Washington can boast the best oyster stew around. Smooth and savory oyster stew has been a staple among Northwest shellfish growers for generations. But it wasn't until the 1950s, when Willapa Bay resident Ed Gruble began marketing canned oyster stew, that this flavorful concoction became a familiar household item.

Gruble left the produce business to become an oysterman in the late 1940s. After studying the ins and outs of the industry, the young entrepreneur eventually quit his job at Coast Oyster Company's South Bend cannery to start his own shellfish plant, the Willapa Bay Oyster Company in 1952. Here, opportunity knocked, in the form of 100,000 gallons of Pacific oyster meats stored in 10-gallon milk cans.

"These were huge oysters, four or five to a pint, and their size made them less desirable for canning," Gruble remembers. "They were just sitting there with no place to go, depressing the market for fresh oysters with their mass."

That's when Gruble came up with the idea of slicing the surplus Pacifics and making them into a canned oyster stew. Devising a winning formula for a canned product, however, proved more difficult than Gruble or his coworkers could have guessed. "You have an oyster with a pH of 6.0 and milk with a pH that's considerably higher, around 6.5," Gruble explains. "Put the two together and it's like a chemistry experiment. The difference causes the milk to curdle and ruin the product." Gruble turned to the region's cheese makers for advice about stabilizing the milk-and-oyster mix. Their advice, which Gruble kept to himself, did the trick.

In 1954, Gruble joined forces with Vernon Hunt of Atherton, California, and Hamilton Dowell of Seattle to form Hilton Seafoods Company, Inc. At its peak, Hilton's 64 employees cranked out 3,000 cases of 8- and 10-ounce cans—some 5,000 gallons of oyster stew every business day.

After 25 years in the business, the czar of oyster stew sold his top-secret formula to the Boston-based New

England Fish Company. That recipe—and the reputation for the best oyster stew—returned to Washington State, when Nefco filed for bankruptcy in 1979, three years after Gruble retired from the oyster biz. Now enjoyed by diners worldwide, oyster stew remains synonymous with life in the Northwest, regardless of its point of manufacture.

"Heinz tried to compete with us, and so did Campbell's Soup, but we had the market for stew all sewn up," Ed Gruble gloats. Primarily East Coast operations, Gruble's competitors lacked supplies of Pacific oysters and were forced to make do with the smaller, less nectar-rich eastern oysters.

acceptance in oyster cocktails and other dishes where its small, round, and completely white flesh could shine.

Having learned from previous bad experiences, the Washington Fisheries Department took steps to prevent any exotic pests from entering state waters along with the seed. They sent two biologists, John Glude and Cedric Lindsay, to oversee the packing operation in Japan and keep a close watch for the Japanese oyster drill, *Ocenebra japonica*, a pest on a par with its Atlantic cousin. Even with such close scrutiny, *Ocenebra* slipped into Willapa Bay and Puget Sound in seed shipments. Regulations governing the transport of oyster shell from bed to bed have since slowed the Japanese drill's predatory advances.

Not every marine invertebrate from Japan has been an enemy of the regional environment. Some, like the Manila clam (*Venerupis japonica*), have been downright welcome and now support a sizeable commercial shellfish industry, limited only by available rearing habitat. But for the most part, the invaders have been harmful, not helpful. High on the list of America's Least Wanted is the carnivorous flatworm *Pseudostylochus*

ostreophagus, first spied in Puget Sound by state shellfish biologist Chuck Woelke, who blew the whistle on this slayer of juvenile native oysters, also presumed to have originated in Japan.

While Japan struggled to reinstate itself as a seed supplier, the oyster god smiled once again on American oystermen, providing them with a more favorable climate and prime water conditions, which combined to yield a profusion of seed in a few of the best oyster bays. One hot spot for spat was discovered by E. N. Steele's son Dick. While on furlough during the war, Dick had returned to his Washington home and spent time scouting for sites where Pacific oyster larvae were most likely to settle on pre-set cultch. His search led him to a prime piece of shoreline property at the head of Dabob Bay off Hood Canal. The Steele family purchased the land in 1945, willing to gamble on Dick's hunch.

Years earlier, shellfish biologists with the Washington Department of Fisheries had begun to systematically study the traits that made certain bays better suited for spat production. Most of their exploration was done by boat in and around Willapa

A RECENT (AND RARE) PRIZE: THE KUMAMOTO OYSTER

CRASSOSTREA SIKAMEA

Named for the Japanese prefecture where this stock was first cultivated, the Kumamoto oyster is a molluscan morsel that has gained a strong following in the Northwest. Originally imported in the late 1940s to replace diminishing supplies of Pacifics and Olympias, these treasures of the intertidal have been adopted by a handful of local growers.

Kumos, as they are known to the trade, have a subtler, more refined flavor than Olympia oysters. Their shells hold considerably more meat—a real plus for seafood connoisseurs.

Unlike the Olympia oyster, this species can't spawn in the comparatively colder waters of Puget Sound and the outer coast. And so, Washington's growers must rely on hatchery-reared stock. This drawback is offset by the fact that Kumamotos are available in all seasons, even in summer when Olys and Pacifics are spawning—an activity that, as a side effect, makes their flesh unappealing to seafood connoisseurs. Kumos take about three years to reach a marketable size of about two inches across.

In the early 1970s, Northwest hatcheries started crossbreeding Kumos with related Pacifics. The resulting Gigamoto "was a watery oyster that didn't have the deep cup of the Kumamoto at all," Anja Robinson of the Hatfield Marine Science Center in Oregon told the *Wall Street Journal*.

When growers and researchers mounted an expedition in 1989 to find fresh, unaltered Kumamoto seedlings from Japan, they returned empty-handed. Alas, after several decades of selective crossbreeding by Japanese shellfish growers, a genetically pure stock no longer exists in the Kumo's native land. For such, Northwest growers must now depend on the descendants of the original imported stocks.

The free-swimming phase is one of several developmental stages in a young oyster's life.

and the waters of Dabob and Quilcene Bays.

"We'd take water samples, near the surface and as far as 30 feet down," says Cedric Lindsay, one of several state biologists involved in the study. "Oyster larvae tend to gravitate to the surface at night and drop down during the daylight hours, so we'd begin our sampling late in the afternoon."

Lindsay's associate, Ron Wesley, augmented sampling with dye and drift studies to determine how water currents would affect spat distribution. He learned that larval abundance and dispersal were influenced by a complicated mixture of winds, weather, tides, and other natural forces.

Biologists and oceanographers discovered that runoff from heavy rains or an exceptional snowmelt could fill the canal with fresh water. Less dense than salt water, the runoff floats at the surface, forming a transparent but visually discernible freshwater lens. This lens focuses solar radiation, transmitting its heat to the water directly beneath it. This causes a layer of warm sea water to build directly below the lens, creating a more nurturing environment for oyster larvae. Strong north

winds would sometimes offset this effect, creating strong surface currents that would carry the larvae far from shore and prevent them from settling down.

Biologists in British Columbia have conducted similar studies of spatfall in Pendrell Sound on East Redonda Island, a sparsely populated landmass in the Strait of Georgia. Spawning in this deep fjord-like inlet has been consistently strong, with only a few less-than-sensational years since the 1950s, when government records of this phenomenon were first kept.

Recognizing the commercial potential of Pendrell, the provincial government declared the sound an oyster seed reserve, equally accessible to anyone, whether a small hobby farmer or large-scale commercial grower. The only restriction to the mass-marketing of this seed has been the sound's isolated geography. Regardless, in some years, the revenue from Pendrell Sound seed sales has been equal to that of oysters, canned or fresh, in all of British Columbia.

In August 1946, the Steeles' gamble paid off. As Dick and the state workers had predicted, the remaining Pacific oysters in Dabob Bay's beds began spawning with gusto, filling the cold sea with ciliated (free-swimming) oyster larvae, ready to settle and grow. Father and son were now prepared to capitalize on the sudden spatfall. In the currents offshore, they anchored a network of floating rafts, each bearing strings of so-called "mother" shell. With these structures, first introduced in Japan, they convinced the bay's abundant oyster larvae to stick around—that is, to affix themselves to the shell strands and metamorphose into cornflake-sized spat.

The Steeles waited until the miniature oysters' shells had become firm enough (a process called "hardening") to withstand being moved back to the culture beds. They now had adequate stock for themselves.

Later, the Steeles leased state-owned tidelands in Dabob Bay, built additional floating racks, and started selling seed to other growers. Many of today's oyster farmers rely on seed from Dick and other growers in northern Hood Canal, where it happens that healthy sets occur about 7 years out of 10. In some years, as many as 50,000 cases of Hood Canal seed have been packaged and sold to growers in the Northwest. After a series of poor seed-growing seasons crippled Japan's shellfish operations in the early 1990s, Hood Canal's "homegrown" seed, now raised indoors in huge hatchery tanks, was shipped overseas to bolster Japanese beds.

At last, seed suppliers from the Miyagi Prefecture were ready to deliver their goods on a grand scale. In the spring of 1947, they shipped nearly 57,000 cases of Pacific oyster seed for planting in Washington, Oregon, British Columbia, and Alaska. Northwest oyster growers could now breathe a collective sigh of relief. With the exception of 1951, when a series of violent winter storms threatened to disrupt Japanese seed shipments, the supply of Pacific oysters would remain consistent for the next 20 years.

Once again, the future looked rosy for Northwest oystermen. However, any sense of security would soon vanish, as a new threat to the industry began to reveal itself. This time, the enemy wasn't an overseas invader or a shortsighted overharvester of shellfish beds back home. Instead, the new culprit was innocently being welcomed along Western coastlines—a villain that oystermen would have to fight harder than ever to defeat.

EATING AT THE ARK

If you visited Nahcotta, Washington, in the 1950s, you wouldn't have dared miss one of the West Coast's best oyster feeds. In those days you could pull up a chair at Lucille Wilson's Ark Café and order the special—fried oysters, all you can eat. While you gazed out the window at the oyster cannery across the road, your waitress would have brought you an amazing meal. Shrimp cocktail or clam chowder for starters, followed by a salad. Then came your platter, a mountain of crispy, golden-fried oysters (you could ask for more if you could hold 'em!) plus vegetable, toast, coffee, and scrumptious pie a la mode. At the end, if you could still reach your wallet, you would happily pay $3.50.

Today things cost a little more, but the oyster feeds at the Ark are still not to be missed. Since 1981, chefs Jimella Lucas and Nanci Main have operated the Ark Restaurant and Bakery. In their practiced hands, oyster cooking is a fine art, but they've also kept tradition alive with their "Willapa Oyster Platter." Jimella recommends extra small Willapa Bay oysters, lightly breaded and fried to perfection.

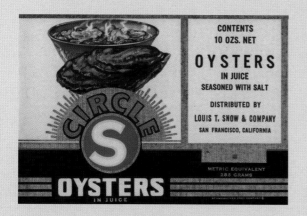

THE ARK FRIED OYSTERS

24 extra small Pacific oysters, shells well scrubbed
4 eggs
2 cups milk
2 cups all-purpose flour
2 to 3 cups extra fine cracker meal or bread crumbs
1/3 cup vegetable oil or butter

Shuck the oysters and drain them in a colander. In a medium bowl, prepare an egg wash by beating together the eggs and milk. Put the flour in a large plate and the cracker meal or bread crumbs in a large baking dish. Working with 8 to 10 oysters at a time, dust the oysters lightly with the flour, patting to remove the excess, then place them in the egg wash for 3 to 5 minutes. With a slotted spoon, lift oysters from the egg wash and allow excess to drain off, then put the oysters in the cracker meal or bread crumbs and thoroughly coat them. Repeat with the remaining oysters. This can be done up to an hour ahead. Keep the breaded oysters refrigerated until you are ready to cook them. In a 10-inch skillet or flat-top griddle, heat the oil over medium-high heat. Brown the oysters on one side, turn and brown them on the other side, then lift with slotted spoon and drain on paper towels. Serve on lettuce leaves with a lemon wedge and your favorite tartar sauce. Makes 4 servings.

(From: Jimella Lucas, The Ark Café, Nahcotta, Washington, 2001)

A regional favorite: Lonny's Oyster Stew (page 125). Pacific oysters, water, and a pinch of salt—the contents of cans from California (left) and Washington (below) are refreshingly simple. A more complicated formula is required for canned oyster stew (page 124).

IN A STEW OVER YOU

Pacific oysters grow plump and sometimes too large to be suitable for canning or serving on the half shell. Thank goodness for oyster stew. Sliced oysters, snug in a rich stew, are healthful, nutritious, and tasty, warming you to the tips of your toes on a fall or winter evening. When Lucille Wilson wasn't frying oysters, you can bet she was stewing them. Her cooking was famous around Willapa Bay. Her recipe and Nancy Lloyd's were obtained at the Oysterville Interpretive Center on Willapa Bay.

LUCILLE WILSON'S OYSTER STEW

1 jar Pacific oysters (10 ounces)
1¼ cups water
1 teaspoon to 1 tablespoon finely chopped onion
2 tablespoons all-purpose flour
2 cups milk (as rich as your diet allows)
Butter
Salt and pepper
Tabasco (optional)

Drain the oysters and rinse them in a colander. Put the oysters in a large saucepan, add the water and onion, and boil for 3 to 5 minutes. Scoop out the oysters with a slotted spoon and set aside to cool, saving the broth. Cut the oysters into small pieces and return them to the broth. Put the flour in a small dish and add 1 to 2 tablespoons water, stirring to make a paste. Stir the flour paste into the broth and bring to a boil, stirring to blend and thicken the stew. Add the milk and a lump of butter. Season to taste with salt and pepper, and a dash of Tabasco if you like. Makes 4 servings.

If you suffer from lactose intolerance, Oysterville's Nancy Lloyd offers a tasty variation on Lucille's recipe.

NANCY'S VARIATION OF OYSTER STEW

Drain and rinse the oysters as above. Put them in the saucepan with $3/4$ to 1 cup water and 2 tablespoons finely chopped onion and cook as noted. Remove the oysters to cool, saving the broth. Cut the oysters into small pieces and return them to the broth. Thicken the broth as above, using rice flour in place of the all-purpose flour if you prefer. Bring to boil and add 1 can (14.5 ounces) full strength chicken broth. Season to taste with salt and pepper.

Looking for something even heartier, with a bit of a European flair? Search no farther than Washington's own Port Townsend, where Lonny Ritter serves it up thick and sprinkled with parsley.

LONNY'S OYSTER STEW

$1/4$ pound pancetta or bacon, cut in $1/4$ inch dice
2 fennel bulbs, trimmed and chopped
2 medium leeks, white parts only, rinsed and chopped
1 teaspoon fennel seed, crushed
6 cups half-and-half or milk
3 jars (10 ounces each) oysters and their liquor (about 1 quart)
$3/4$ cup chopped Italian parsley
1 tablespoon Pernod, sambuca, or other anise-flavor liqueur (not sweet)
Salt and pepper
1 to 2 tablespoons butter or margarine

Put the pancetta in a 5- to 6-quart pan over medium heat. Add the fennel, leeks, and fennel seed and cook, stirring often, until limp but not browned, about 5 minutes. Add the half-and-half or milk and the oysters and their liquor. Increase the heat to medium-high and stir often just until the stew is hot but not boiling, about 4 minutes. Stir in $1/2$ cup of the parsley, the anise liqueur, and salt and pepper to taste. Ladle the stew into bowls and sprinkle with the remaining parsley, then add a dot of butter to each. Makes 6 servings.

(From: *Sunset Magazine*, August 1997)

6. FROM BOOM TO BUST AND BACK

Used to be we had wooden boats and iron men. Now we got iron boats and wooden men.

—*Jim Kemmer, in* Memories of our Past: An Anthology of Stories from the Long Beach Peninsula, *1999*

Historically, water pollution has been the oyster farmer's worst enemy. In the early 1900s, deteriorating water quality hastened the demise of shellfishing on several of the East Coast's more productive embayments. On the West Coast in the 1930s, the degraded condition of San Francisco Bay caused northern California's once-burgeoning eastern oyster industry to collapse. In Washington and Oregon, pollution has encroached on a number of oyster-growing areas. The entire eastern shore of Puget Sound, an 80-mile stretch that includes the cities of Olympia, Tacoma, Seattle, and Everett, has been closed to shellfish harvesting—and is likely to remain that way for many years to come. As of this writing, 17 of Washington's 106 commercial shellfish-growing areas have been classified by state health authorities as threatened by pollution. In at least two of these sites, the oysters must be moved to clean water and allowed to purge themselves of pollutants before they are sold.

Shoveling oysters into shucking house bins (opposite). In Washington, oyster growers' water quality woes went public in the 1960s. Billboards in Bellingham (below) warned that all was not well.

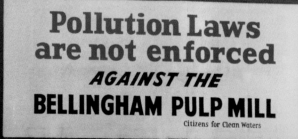

**Pollution Laws
are not enforced**
AGAINST THE
BELLINGHAM PULP MILL
Citizens for Clean Waters

Sunset Outdoor

The Northwest's rapid growth in the 20th century resulted in numerous disputes over shoreline uses and abuses (above). Some of these conflicts have been resolved, while others are far from being settled in this century. Recent battles revolve around aquatic recreation (opposite) and shellfish farming.

If levels of water-borne contamination are extremely high, even the hardiest oysters will suffer and eventually die. Should this happen, the oysterman may be out of luck, long after a polluter has been identified and measures taken to clean up the mess. That's because many pollutants, including pesticides, oil products, and heavy metals from industrial processes, are extremely persistent. They can bind to bottom sediments, slowly releasing their deadly residuals into the marine environment and causing considerable harm to any fish and shellfish that come in contact with them. Efforts to clean up contaminated sediments in some heavily urbanized bays have been known to extend over decades.

In the 1920s, when much of Puget Sound's shoreline was still undeveloped, Northwest shellfish farmers first expressed concern over pollution—in this case the liquid waste from pulp mills adjoining their waterfront parcels. In a letter submitted to the state Supervisor of Fisheries in June 1926, the Olympia Oyster Growers' Association warned that such waste "if permitted to go into tide waters or the streams flowing therein will destroy or be highly deleterious to fish, clams, oysters, and other sea life."

The main component of the effluent was what environmental scientists call sulfite waste liquors—the watery, rust-colored residues of the papermaking process. "When the tide was low, the beaches took on the odor of a cesspool," wrote Humphrey Nelson, describing the effect of those liquors on his oyster beds. "Eighty percent of the oysters were dead or dying" from exposure to this caustic industrial effluent, he claimed.

In the 1930s, after failing to persuade state officials to stem the mills' potentially poisonous outflow, oystermen in Shelton took action on their own. They filed a lawsuit against the local pulp mills for polluting their bay. The suit was settled out of court, and the mills got the message—to be more clandestine about waste disposal. "The more politically conscious companies had their mills try to release the most visible pollutants at night," observed Daniel Jack Chasan in *The Water Link: A History of Puget Sound as a Resource.*

Despite a brief slow-down during the early years of World War II, the pulp mills continued to pollute shellfish beds with their sulfurous ooze. In 1957, oyster grower Ed Gruble wrote a letter to the *Seattle Post-Intelligencer* newspaper, claiming that "Puget Sound has almost become a 'marine desert'…75 percent of the raw liquor still goes directly into Bellingham Bay, and the bay for a considerable distance from the pulp mill is black as ink."

The tender of 800 acres of prime oyster habitat on Samish Bay, Gruble had much at risk. He became a founding member of Citizens for Clean Water, a grassroots organization with a single cause—stopping the mills from polluting Puget Sound. "We tried to pass an initiative that would've taxed the industry 50 cents a gallon to clean up our bays," Gruble recollects. "Of course the opposition was strong—a network of 28 pulp mills, each with its team of attorneys and public relations men. We didn't stand a chance, and the initiative failed."

Gruble and others repeatedly testified before Congress about oysters and water quality issues, eventually inspiring federal legislators to enact the Clean Water Act of 1972. Under the terms of this act, pulp mills and other shoreline industries are now required to monitor the quality of wastewater emissions and, if they exceed federal clean water standards, to take corrective

measures before releasing the fouled effluent into public waters.

But even with the Clean Water Act, Northwest oyster beds and their tenders remained vulnerable to the effects of water pollution. Federal regulations have substantially curbed pollution from so-called "point" sources—sewer pipes, industrial wastewater outlets, and other discrete sources of water pollution. However, they had failed to address equally insidious "nonpoint" sources. Unlike point sources, nonpoint sources of pollution lack easily identified discharge sites. Diverse and difficult to control, these are often linked to our daily activities. Disease-causing bacteria from failing septic systems and animal waste from feed lots and farm fields are among the most common threats to shellfish posed by nonpoint sources of pollution.

Not that the oysters themselves seem to care. In fact, as filter-feeders, they may benefit from the nutrients in fecal matter washed into the sea. However, people who eat the shellfish may suffer. Public health agencies will declare shellfish from such polluted waters unsuitable for collection and sale. Growers of oysters in these waters must wait for the appropriate government agency to determine the source of the fecal contamination and take action to stem its sickly flow. Weeks, months, and years may pass before a shellfish beach is recertified as safe. In the meantime, growers must find other locations for raising oysters—or seek supplemental sources of income—until conditions change.

The sum total of nonpoint pollution can far outweigh the collective contributions of pulp mills or other point sources today. Only after 1987, when Congress reauthorized the Clean Water Act, were provisions to control nonpoint sources incorporated into the federal scheme.

Population growth throughout the Northwest has compounded the potential for polluting commercial oyster beds. This is especially true in small coastal towns, which often lack the infrastructure and planning expertise to manage such growth. In many of these communities, oyster farmers have become outspoken advocates, reminding newcomers that theirs is a time-honored occupation, inextricably linked to the shoreline and to pristine sources of sea water.

HELP FROM HATCHERIES

Recent advances in aquaculture have offset the problem of worsening water quality. Perhaps the greatest boon to oyster growers has been the availability of hatchery stock—oysters reared under controlled conditions for planting on Northwest tideflats.

The concept of breeding oysters in tanks and tubs is not new. In North America, the technology can be traced back nearly 150 years to Johns Hopkins University in Baltimore, where researchers successfully spawned a batch of eastern oysters under laboratory conditions. But it wasn't until the 1920s that anyone tried to put oyster-breeding techniques to work on a grand scale. Spearheading that effort on the West Coast was none other than biologist Trevor Kincaid. With help from shellfishers E. N. Steele and J. C. Barnes, he constructed a makeshift laboratory at the Rock Point Oyster Company plant on Samish Bay. The oyster larvae for his experiments were kept in a large beer barrel, inspiring Kincaid to quip that his oysters were fond of

the sudsy brew. According to Steele, the larvae "danced around as though greatly stimulated." The youngsters "lived longer than in previous trials but soon faded out."

Undaunted, Kincaid moved his laboratory to Willapa Bay in 1926. Here he built several spawning ponds near Naselle, and stocked them with adult Pacific oysters. The professor waited, watched, and eventually terminated the experiment after nothing notable happened. In Nahcotta during the 1950s, Kincaid and his companions again tried to breed oysters under controlled conditions. This time they constructed a huge, concrete pond with a roof to shield the spawning shellfish from the elements. After several years without results, the pond and its spawned-out

Early experiments in oyster breeding produced sperm and eggs (above) but few viable offspring. Trevor Kincaid's pioneering efforts in the 1920s (below left) led to the successful oyster hatcheries of today.

At Taylor Shellfish's hatchery in Quilcene (above), a technician inspects one of several large tanks filled with young oysters. Modern hatchery technologies (opposite) have markedly changed the complexion of the Northwest oyster industry.

occupants were abandoned. Workers with the Washington Department of Fisheries continued to keep the hatchery concept alive, operating a small but functional shellfish breeding facility at their Point Whitney lab.

Ten years later in his Milford, Connecticut, laboratory, biologist Victor Loosanoff of the federal Bureau of Commercial Fisheries proved to the world that spawning oysters indoors was no pipe dream. His success with the artificial propagation of shellfish inspired several others to open experimental oyster hatcheries on the West Coast. Two businessmen, William Budge and Charles Black, built what may be the first of these facilities at Pigeon Point, south of San Francisco. Around the same time, the Engman Oyster Company built its hatchery on Washington's Liberty Bay. Although the Engman hatchery eventually closed, one of its former employees, Lee Hanson, moved to Netarts Bay, Oregon, and opened the Whiskey Creek Oyster Hatchery in 1979. That operation continues to supply Northwest growers with oyster seed.

Coast Seafood (formerly Coast Oyster) is also credited with two of the earliest hatcheries in the Northwest, at Nahcotta and Quilcene, Washington. For some unexplained reason, the Nahcotta hatchery never took off, but the Quilcene facility has done remarkably well. It currently ranks as the largest shellfish hatchery in the world. Taylor Shellfish also built a hatchery on Dabob Bay, within a few minutes' drive of Coast's oyster-spawning facility on Quilcene Bay. Other hatchery operations have been established at Bay Center, Totten Inlet, San Juan Island, and Lummi Island. The Washington Department of Fish and Wildlife also runs a hatchery, primarily for research purposes, at its Point Whitney facility on Hood Canal.

On paper, it doesn't take much to operate a hatchery—just a few adult oysters, some containers of sea water to hold them and their brood, and sources of oxygen, food, and warmth to pamper the lot. By gradually raising the temperature of their water over a period of six to eight weeks, the adult oysters can be tricked into thinking it's spring—the season for spawning. After the oysters have spawned, their fertilized eggs are transferred to other seawater-filled vessels. It takes 12 to 20 days for the eggs to develop into larvae that are ready to settle onto a cultch medium (usually crushed oyster shell). The cultch with seed oysters attached is then shipped to growers throughout the Pacific Northwest.

Oysters that are unattached to so-called "mother shell" can also be produced by hatcheries. By adding epinephrine (a naturally occurring hormone also known as adrenaline) to the water, the swimming larvae are stimulated to drop to the bottom of their tank and continue to metamorphose without cementing themselves to a cultch medium. Because they grow individually instead of in clumps, the cultchless oysters are preferred by growers of single oysters for the half-shell trade.

Some hatcheries specialize in the production of "eyed" larvae, named for the minute speck of pigmented tissue—a light-sensitive spot—in the middle of each youngster's flesh. These oysters have yet to settle and attach themselves to shell. Strained from the water of a hatchery tank, the larvae are wrapped in damp cheesecloth, kept cool in a small ice chest, and shipped by the millions to customers around the world. On

arrival, they can be transferred to a settling tank and allowed to fasten themselves to cultch media. Through this revolutionary process, called remote setting, oyster growers are now assured of an even more reliable and economical source of seed. Cultchless seed is also more sanitary—considerably less prone to harbor diseases or exotic parasites. Supposedly, the viability of transporting larval oysters in this fashion was discovered by accident, after the hatchery crew at Coast Seafood's Quilcene facility left a batch of larvae drying on the screens of a separating sieve for several hours. "The technicians who left the larvae on the screens may not have survived, but from their error came a new way to ship larvae," quipped Lee Hanson at a Washington Sea Grant–sponsored workshop in 1991. Later studies have shown that larvae could be refrigerated and stored for up to eight days without impairing their ability to settle and grow.

Hatchery technologies have made it more convenient for the citizens of Alaska to grow Pacific oysters on their southeastern shores. Pacific oysters do not reproduce in the cold waters of Alaska. As a result, oyster farmers must buy their spat from hatcheries in Washington, Oregon, and northern California. By seeding their beaches with the out-of-state shellfish, Alaskan growers can contend with the brief growing season, from late June to early September. Because many of Alaska's estuaries are filled seasonally with high-quality plankton, the oysters in some beds grow at a similar rate to those in warmer waters of British Columbia and Washington, according to Raymond RaLonde, a University of Alaska aquaculture specialist.

A NEW BIVALVE IS BORN

Within a spawning tank, the biggest and best specimens can be crossbred to produce faster growing and more robust oyster strains. Many of today's oyster strains have come from such molluscan matchmaking. A few of these hatchery-born bivalves have been recruited in the war against what is commonly known as summer mortality—a lethal but as-yet undiagnosed shellfish disease. For nearly five decades this mysterious seasonal ailment has plagued certain Pacific oyster beds, destroying from 70 to 90 percent of their shelled occupants in a matter of weeks. The first outbreaks were observed in the summer of 1958, a year characterized by the return of the warming El Niño ocean current. Most were confined to beds at the heads of a few bays in coastal California and southern Puget Sound. But in succeeding years, the unexplained oyster deaths continued to mount, and summer mortality became progressively more widespread. The blight was soon wiping out beds at the mouths of bays and other previously unreported locales. Even worse, summer mortalities were occurring earlier in the growing season, making it more difficult to rear Pacific oysters with each passing year.

Throughout the 1960s, shellfish biologists toiled to establish the cause of summer mortality and to slow its spread. Circumstantial evidence tied the disease to two factors: changing ocean conditions and the stressed physiologies of mature Pacific oysters in

summer months. The warm, nutrient-rich seas of summertime are more nurturing for bacteria, viruses, and other disease-causing organisms. Ironically, these same months coincide with the period when mature oysters have expended their energies to produce eggs and sperm. Some proposed that these "spent" oysters were most susceptible to secondary invasions by water-borne pathogens.

Unable to identify the actual disease organism, researchers in the early 1980s concentrated on producing oysters that could withstand the mystery killer's attacks. In experimental hatcheries, they

At his University of Washington laboratory, Professor Kenneth Chew and his graduate students perfected the triploid Pacific oyster—a shellfish with three sets of chromosomes instead of two. Although triploidy hasn't fully lived up to its promise, there have been many benefits from Chew's genetically well-endowed bivalve.

crossbred the survivors from summer mortality-ravaged beds in the hope of creating an invincible strain. Unfortunately the oyster that was born from such broodstock was lean and slow growing—considerably less desirable for commercial use.

A second, more beneficial oyster was unveiled in the mid-1980s by University of Washington professor Kenneth Chew. Assisted by graduate students Standish Allen Jr. and Sandra Downing and inspired by a similar project at the University of Maine, Chew created a genetically altered triploid oyster—a mutant shellfish with three sets of chromosomes in each body cell instead of the usual two. Like other triploid animals, this shellfish oddity was incapable of producing eggs or sperm. Unlike the meat of ordinary Pacific oysters, which usually becomes runny or chalky during the reproductive season, the flesh of the so-called "sexless" oyster would remain flavorful throughout the year. Triploid oysters are advantageous for other reasons: they grow more rapidly, are sweeter tasting, and, while less fattening, are higher in protein than their diploid kin.

The first batches of triploid Pacific oysters were created in 1984, by subjecting fertilized eggs to from 5,000 to 10,000 pounds of pressure per square inch—a crushing load equivalent to that withstood by the best equipped submarine, five miles down on the sea floor. The following year, Chew and associates adopted an alternate method, using the cytachalasin B, an antibiotic secreted by several species of fungi, to produce the desired effects. Oyster larvae are briefly bathed in this chemical, then transferred to ordinary hatchery tanks. Some of the oysters die from this process, but the ones that survive are later planted in Northwest beds. Current attempts to produce triploids from diploids (oysters with the usual two sets of chromosomes) bred with tetraploids (aberrant oysters with four chromosome sets) may eliminate the need for mutagenic chemicals.

Hatchery technologies for making triploids aren't foolproof: a small percentage of the oyster larvae remain diploids even after being exposed to cytachalasin B. Regardless, these genetically altered bivalves have revolutionized the oyster industry. Today, about a third of all canned and jarred oysters are triploid. A similar

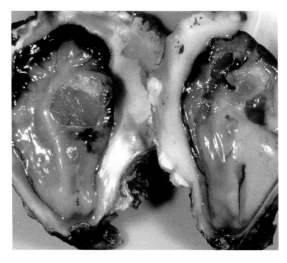

VACATIONING SHELLFISH

Which of these Pacific oysters (left) is a triploid? Answer: the one with the bigger adductor muscle on the left.

Hatchery technologies continue to evolve at a brisk clip. Many hatchery owners have recently found a way to give their seed stock a boost, dramatically reducing the time for the oysters to grow to the size for planting Northwest beds. The secret? Send the seed on a Hawaiian vacation.

For Taylor Shellfish, this bold maneuver involved opening a facility in Kona on the island of Hawaii. A key feature of this new site is the intense, year-round tropical sunlight, which ensures an ample supply of diatoms for the young oysters to eat. Another is warm water, a second stimulus for rapid shellfish growth.

"On Kona, we're set up to take advantage of the effluent from a former ocean thermal energy plant," explains Bill Dewey, director of marketing for Taylor Shellfish. Built by the Natural Energy Laboratory of Hawaii Authority (NELHA), the plant was designed to have one intake drawing cold sea water from a depth of about 2,000 feet and another drawing warmer sea water

technique is being used to create sexless geoducks, the biggest of North America's burrowing clams.

The creation of the triploid oyster proved significant for an altogether different reason. When the University of Washington tried to patent its process in April 1987, its application was turned down in federal court. However, the application prompted a landmark ruling that higher animals—not just lowly bacteria—were patentable. This ruling has prompted interest among biotechnology researchers and concern among activists and in Congress about the implications of genetic engineering.

from the surface. When the cold and warm sea water came in contact, any gases dissolved in the water were released. The gases were then funneled through a series of turbines, generating electricity for the island's homes and businesses. As it turned out, the plant never produced enough power to pay for its construction and maintenance costs. Instead, NELHA is leasing the site to Taylor and other fish and shellfish companies.

"To our seed oysters, it's like being in a big bathtub, with separate taps for hot and cold water," Dewey says. "We can adjust those taps, making sure the oysters are supplied with sea water at the optimum temperature for growth."

To take advantage of this system, Taylor's hatchery workers routinely send 20 million seed oysters to Kona in a small six-pack beer cooler. Three to six months later, when it's starting to warm up in Washington's waters, their counterparts in Kona ship the oysters back.

The returning shellfish are thumbnail-sized, perfect for planting on Taylor Shellfish's properties. "We get a real jump start on the growing season," Dewey offers, "and we don't have to spend so much money on feeding our seed oysters or heating their water in winter months."

Despite its many obvious advantages, hatchery-supplied seed was slow to win acceptance among growers in the Northwest. Perhaps they perceived this new source as unnatural—the Frankensteinian offspring, sired in the lab and unleashed on the outside world. It's more probable that they had grown overly accustomed to seed imports from Japan, augmented with wild supplies, collected at local beaches. Like most farmers throughout history, the oystermen were by and large a conservative lot, predisposed to wait and see if the new hatchery seed was worth its asking price.

Only in the early 1980s, when French oyster growers began buying Japanese seed in bulk, causing its price to skyrocket, did many Northwesterners become convinced that hatcheries were the way to go. Judging from production figures for Washington, these new sources of seed caused the Northwest oyster industry to once again boom, nearly doubling the yearly output of oyster meat—from 600,000 gallons in 1980 to about 1,100,000 in 1987. The price of meats almost tripled, from $6.75 per gallon of canned oysters in 1980 to nearly $17 per gallon of fresh oysters, at the decade's end.

Today, it's hard to calculate how many cultched and cultchless oysters are purchased by Northwest growers each year. Chances are, the figure approaches 40 billion. "We've gone from producing one billion larvae in 1979 to 28 billion per year now," Coast Seafood's now-retired hatchery manager, Jim Donaldson, told readers of the Jefferson County, Washington, *Leader* newspaper in July 2000. "We started this as a pilot project with a staff of two; now there are 25."

Yet even with help from hatcheries, modern-day farmers must labor long and hard to eke out a living from their oyster beds. In recent years, many growers have sought to suppress a population explosion of blue mud shrimp (*Upogebia pugetensis*) and bay ghost shrimp (*Neotrypaea californiensis*) in the tidelands. Both shrimp species are ambitious tunnelers, constructing elaborate burrows in the substrate. The blue mud shrimp's burrow is a long tube with two openings, two to four feet apart. The bay ghost shrimp's is more convoluted, with numerous side chambers and turn-arounds. Ejected sediment from these excavations can bury juvenile oysters. As if that weren't bad enough, sometimes the tunneling severely softens the substrate, causing the oysters to slowly sink from sight. Oysters and their cultivators aren't the only ones to suffer: some studies suggest the unchecked activities of burrowing shrimp can reduce the natural species diversity of oyster beds by 80 to 95 percent.

What triggered the shrimp explosion is not fully understood. Some theorize that the decline of shrimp-eating chum salmon and green and white sturgeon may have released these

One of several species of burrowing shrimp, the four-inch-long *Neotrypaea californiensis* can cause big trouble for oyster growers in Oregon and Washington.

OLYMPIA OYSTERS STAGE A COMEBACK

After decades of neglect, Olympia oysters are again drawing the attention of shellfishers in the Pacific Northwest. Most of this interest, though, is not food-related. Instead, it's focused on the little oysters' big role as a keystone species—an organism on which many other species depend. The fissures created by the smaller, more densely packed clusters of Olympia oyster shells provide safe havens and sites of attachment for tiny, niche-dwelling marine fish, invertebrates, and plants. Recent studies suggest that Olympia oysters support richer and more diverse underwater communities than do similar-sized clusters of farmed Pacific oysters. Members of these communities often include the prey of larger marine animals—from hefty Pacific salmon to gargantuan humpback whales. Olympia oysters themselves are eaten by many animals incapable of swallowing the bigger, thicker-shelled Pacific oysters. One early settler of south Puget Sound wrote of taking 18 Olympia oysters from the craw of a single sea duck.

Add cultural significance to the list of reasons for favoring native Olympia oysters over nonnative Pacifics. Tribes in California, Oregon, Washington, British Columbia, and Alaska harvested Olympia oysters for thousands of years before other oyster species were introduced to the Northwest. Returning Olympia oysters to their historic habitats is "a very powerful thing to do," according to Genny Rogers, cultural resources technician for the Skokomish Indian Tribe, the original inhabitants of Hood Canal, Washington. "It's part of our identity, our world," she says.

Workers with the Washington Department of Fish and Wildlife recently joined forces with the nonprofit Puget Sound Restoration Fund, the for-profit Taylor Shellfish Company, and the Skokomish, Squaxin Island, and Suquamish Indian tribes to put Olympia oysters on the beaches where they once abounded. In early 1999, oysters were collected from a locale near Quilcene and brought to the Point Whitney Shellfish Laboratory in nearby Brinnon. Here they were spawned under controlled conditions. The resulting oyster larvae settled on Pacific oyster shell, which was later scattered along in tidal channels on the Skokomish Reservation. Ideally, the offspring of these oysters will gradually reestablish themselves throughout Hood Canal. Olympia oysters from other sources are also being used to replenish south and central Puget Sound.

Similar efforts are now under way in Oregon's Netarts, Yaquina, and Alsea Bays. After discovering several small colonies of native oysters in a slough near Redwood City, California, shellfish biologists may soon get into the Olympia act. Another relic population has been located in Alameda. Whether these are true California natives or merely the descendants of oysters brought down in the 1850s from Willapa Bay has not been established.

Native Olympia oysters have always been popular, even at the height of the Pacific oyster's popularity in the 1940s, when this photograph of an Olympia, Washington, restaurant was taken. In more recent years, they've been recognized as cultural icons and important components of regional marine ecosystems.

Biologists from the
Washington Department of
Fish and Wildlife monitor
burrowing shrimp to better
assess the extent of
their spread.

oyster pests from predation pressure. Even less clear is the best method for controlling the shrimp. Oyster growers have used an array of nonchemical measures— from covering their beds with tarpaper (as was done in the late 1800s) to rolling them out of the ground. The founder of Willapa's Jolly Roger oyster company, John Wiegardt, tried this second approach in the 1960s. He acquired a motorpool of surplus Army vehicles, including a half-track for lugging an old water tank across his shrimp-infested tideflats. "It got rid of the shrimp, alright," says John's cousin Lee Wiegardt, "but it also got rid of the oysters! It disrupted the substrate, and the silt just floated away. It didn't leave anything for the oysters to grow on!"

Currently the most effective control measure is the pesticide carbaryl, a chemical compound sold under the trade name Sevin. But because carbaryl acts as a broad-spectrum pesticide, if sprayed indiscriminately, it can kill small fish, juvenile crabs, and other creatures that share oyster beds. On the other hand, there is some evidence that carbaryl-treated grounds may actually invite young Dungeness crabs and other many forms of life to make homes among the oyster shells. The Washington Department of Ecology limits its use to exposed oyster beds during daylight tides in July and August, when migrating salmon are least likely to be swimming within spraying range. Before they can be issued a permit to apply carbaryl, oyster farmers in Washington must certify that their oyster beds are severely infested with shrimp and that they have filed a plan for safe storage, use, and disposal of the compound. In Oregon, carbaryl has been outlawed entirely, causing some growers to grumble that the government has assisted in the destruction of several formerly productive oyster bays. Shrimp-created deserts cover 20,000 acres in Willapa Bay, and with fewer than 10,000 acres of tideland in oyster production, every acre counts.

Haunted by HABs

Even more puzzling is the recent increase in harmful algal blooms, or HABs as they are called by marine scientists. Occasionally, oceanic conditions favor one species of algae over the others, causing this species to multiply and reach such high concentrations that the water becomes tinged by its cells—a phenomenon commonly called a "red tide." Sometimes the algae that bloom are producers of natural poisons. Some of these are considered among the most toxic substances known to humankind. Because of the algal abundance, these toxins can accumulate in the tissues of oysters and other shellfish that filter-feed. While the toxins do not hurt the shellfish, people who eat the tainted meat can experience tingling sensations, memory loss, shortness of breath, and flu-like symptoms. Some unfortunate diners have been known to die from the effects.

"There are at least five different kinds of toxic algae in Washington's waters," offers Jack Wekell, a research chemist and specialist in marine toxins, with the National Oceanic and Atmospheric Administration in Seattle. "We've been fortunate," he says. "No deaths from shellfish poisoning in over 50 years, and the few cases of illness have been among recreational shellfish harvesters, oblivious to the dangers of HABs."

Not every Northwest state and province has such a spotless record. In Alaska between 1997 and 2000, three deaths and dozens of illnesses were attributed to the consumption of HABs-tainted shellfish by recreational harvesters. Since 1980, at least 183 cases of HABs-related sickness have been reported in the four West Coast states.

Wekell attributes his state's safety record to its aggressive shellfish-monitoring program and to safeguards like the toll-free telephone hotline for recreational shellfish harvesters, which offers daily updates on HABs-affected beaches in coastal areas. Commercial operations in Washington are extremely well monitored, he notes. Oyster farming operations are required to submit samples for inspection by the state Department of Health. Should there be cause for concern, the department can close the commercial and recreational fisheries until further notice.

Such closures can have serious impacts on the shellfish industry, sometimes expressed in millions of dollars in lost revenues for oyster growers in Washington state. In late October 1991, when domoic acid, a toxin from the diatom *Pseudo-nitzschia,* was identified in razor clams and other shellfish harvested on the Pacific Ocean coast, Washington State Department of Health officials took immediate action, first closing the razor clam fishery and then the Dungeness crab fishery until further notice. Health officials in Oregon followed suit, also closing their state's coastal beaches to commercial and recreational harvesters.

The closures remained in effect for about two months, resulting in lost revenues totaling $23 million to $28 million for the two states. Washington's shellfish processors experienced a 50 percent decline in sales and a price drop of 20 percent from the previous year, for losses of around $7.2 million. Although there was no evidence that oysters accumulated domoic acid during this period, coastal oyster farming operations also suffered. According to data compiled by Washington Sea Grant Program, the state's oyster growers lost around

$2.17 million in sales, just because of the public's unfounded fears about eating domoic acid-laden meat. Oyster sales on the Washington coast dropped 10 to 20 percent, with wholesale prices falling 5 to 12 percent.

Coastal Washington's oyster growers were similarly hard-hit by a 1997 bloom of *Alexandrium*—the marine alga associated with paralytic shellfish poisoning—on the coast and in southern Puget Sound. Revenue losses from the closure in response to the bloom on the coast approached the $7 million mark after a mere two to three weeks. Also in southern Puget Sound, where closures remained in effect for two months, growers lost out, bringing the total to around $8 million in lost revenue. One Puget Sound farmer of oysters and clams estimated his losses at $5,000 per week. Sobering by themselves, these figures don't take into account the hundreds of people laid off during this or other closures.

The 1997 closures occurred in November—at a time when shellfish farmers in Willapa Bay and nearby Grays Harbor typically make between 25 and 35 percent of their sales for the year. Holiday-inspired sales were impacted by as much as 50 percent. Months afterward, shellfish farmers and their employees were still striving to regain their market share.

At least one recent study suggests that the world's coastal waters may be experiencing an increase in the number and type of HABs. No one can say with certainty if this increase is attributable to natural cycles or human-caused effects. More species of harmful algae exist in the Northwest than in any other part of the country. With more at stake than most waterfront laborers, oyster growers throughout the Northwest are asking the same basic questions—when and where will the next toxic bloom take place and for how long will it shut down their industry?

The income from oyster shucking (opposite) is lost when a harmful algal bloom occurs, and shellfish beds are closed.

WARNING . . .
TOXIC SHELLFISH

SHELLFISH FROM THIS AREA ARE UNSAFE TO EAT DUE TO PARALYTIC SHELLFISH TOXIN. DO NOT EAT CLAMS, OYSTERS, MUSSELS OR SCALLOPS.

In the 1960s, Lee Wiegardt struggled to keep his cannery competitive. Although no longer canning oysters, his company, Wiegardt Brothers, Inc., is still a strong force in the industry.

MOVING FORWARD AND BACK

Postwar years found Northwest oystermen struggling with yet another foe: foreign competition. To resolve a dispute over rights to shared salmon stocks in the northeast Pacific Ocean, the U.S. had entered into a treaty with Russia, Japan, and Korea. As part of the agreement, these nations removed their sizeable commercial fishing fleets from what had then been established as U.S. territorial waters. In return, the three foreign governments were compensated for revenue lost to their fleets. Korea received financial aid and technical assistance to sell its farm-raised Pacific oysters to American consumers, and, within months of the agreement, U.S. markets were flooded with imports of smoked and stewed oysters in colorfully labeled cans.

Seafood processors in the Northwest could not compete with the low-cost Asian product, canned at a fraction of the cost of domestic processing. At the time, the wholesale price for a carton (48 10-ounce cans) of oysters from Willapa Bay sold for about $14. "The

Koreans were selling their cartons of canned oysters on the open market for $5.65, and that figure included shipping costs and import duty. We were powerless to compete," Lee Wiegardt laments.

Wiegardt's accountant advised him to file for bankruptcy. Rather than dismantle his historic family business, he elected to try canning oyster stew, using his supplies of Pacific oysters from locally owned beds. Again, Wiegardt's enterprise was undercut by Korean shellfish processors, who by now had begun shipping frozen meat for oyster stew. Once more, the price of oysters fell sharply. Like the shellfish they had once canned, the owners of Willapa Bay's processing plants were now in hot water. Unable to pay their employees, most were forced to discontinue their canning operations. Today, only a few small-scale oyster canneries exist in the Northwest, mostly meeting the needs of tourists and fanciers of specialty foods.

Foreign trade might have finished off the entire oyster industry in the Northwest, were it not for the federal Lacey Act. Enacted in 1900, this legislation was originally intended to halt the commercial exploitation of wildlife—a concern at a time when the passenger pigeon and other game birds had been pushed to the brink of extinction by largely unregulated hunting. The act also banned the importation of any insects or other wildlife that might threaten crop production and horticulture. Fortunately for oyster growers, this prohibition extended to imports of live oysters from Korea. In the 1960s, these bivalves had been diagnosed as carriers of a haplosporidian parasite—a microscopic organism linked to MSX, a deadly oyster disease. As a result, Wiegardt and other oystermen were spared from further face-offs with foreign shellfish farmers.

To remain in business, Northwest growers were now required to retrace the footsteps of oystermen in the decades before World War II. They reinvested in shucking houses and the revitalization of the then-overlooked market for fresh oysters on the half shell. Like their forebears, they put considerable energy into new aquaculture techniques and into finding new buyers for their home-grown treasures from the tideflats.

It has taken years to rebuild the market for oysters from the Pacific Northwest. But as today's oyster

Images from a Washington Industries Series slide show are among the few relics of the post-World War II cannery days. Foreign competitors put an end to this era of mechanization, prompting a return to the days of hand labor and the half-shell trade.

growers will attest, interest in fresh fare is at an all-time high, both nationally and overseas. "We're definitely in the middle of a great oyster renaissance," seafood specialist John Rowley of Seattle told readers of the September 1999 issue of *Wine Spectator* magazine. Indeed, as the magazine pointed out, the resurgence of interest in oysters is yet another sign of a healthy U.S. economy ("Forget the Dow—Keep your eyes on oysters

New Markets for an Old-Timer: the European Flat Oyster

Ostrea edulis

Prized by ancient Romans and Gauls, European flat oysters were introduced to the Northwest in the mid-1970s. They are marketed today as Belon oysters, after their ancestral home, the coastal estuaries of Brittany in France. The same species is known in England as the Dorset or Whitstable oyster— and in all likelihood inspired Jonathan Swift's remark, "He was a bold man that first eat an oyster."

The shell of the European flat is small (1^1/$_2$ to 3^1/$_2$ inches across) and easily distinguished from that of the deeply cupped Kumamoto and its not-too-distant cousin, the Pacific oyster. The taste of its meat is flinty or slightly metallic, similar to the Olympia oyster but much more plump and juicy. As such, these oysters are best paired with Loire Chenin Blanc, Sancerre, or Muscadet wines, according to Sam Gugino of *Wine Spectator* magazine.

A few Northwesterners, including Taylor Shellfish in Shelton, Washington, and Hog Island Oyster Company in Marshall, California, farm European flats. Seed and larvae are sold by the Lummi Indian Nation in Washington, which has operated a hatchery since 1971. With a burgeoning world market for half-shell oysters, the future looks bright for the Belon.

to see how the markets are doing," a banner headline proclaimed). And with the nation becoming more fitness-conscious, oysters and other fresh seafood are more valued than ever before.

In the past decade, many oyster-growing operations have discovered appreciative audiences in other countries as well. A prime example is Taylor Shellfish, which currently supplies 150,000 dozen oysters per year to its wholesale and retail store in Hong Kong. Taylor's other customers include seafood outlets in Japan and Taiwan. They've even sold their Washington-grown European flat oysters to buyers in England and France. Add to this the many shipments of oyster seed they've supplied to growers in Chile, Brazil, Mexico, and South Africa, and one can easily understand how truly global the marketplace for Northwest oysters has become.

Along with current efforts to globalize Northwest oyster stocks, many growers are fostering interest in what are commonly called boutique oysters—gourmet strains, often with names reflecting their bays of origin. "In the old days, we would just market Hood Canal oysters," says Jeff Daniels, president of Marinelli Shellfish in Seattle. "Now you have Hamma Hamma, Sunset Beach, Pleasant Cove, Annas Bay, Little Creek, Dabob Bay—and I'm probably forgetting some."

Many of these oysters come from small-scale farms, which, like regional vineyards, have proliferated throughout the coastal Northwest in the past two decades. Fifty miles north of San Francisco, in the town of Marshall on California's Tomales Bay, the owners of Hog Island Oyster Company raise an assortment of succulent shellfish, including Kumamoto, European flat, and

Oyster growers in Marshal, California (below), now devote their energies to rearing Hog Island Sweetwaters and other gourmet shellfish strains for diners throughout the Northwest.

A landmark on the western shore of Quilcene Bay for three generations, Ray Canterbury's oyster farm closed in 1991. Ray cites his bad back as the primary cause of the closure. But there were many other reasons, including water quality problems, that prompted him to retire. Dan Driscoll (opposite) and his family personify the Northwest's modern oyster farmers—energetic, imaginative, and committed to raising the finest shellfish that money can buy.

eastern oysters. They're especially proud of the one they've named the Hog Island Sweetwater, a Pacific strain that the San Francisco *Chronicle* judged the Best American Oyster in a blind taste test conducted in 1989.

Less ambitious in output but equally important from a historic perspective is Oysterville Sea Farms, whose base of operations is a 70-year-old shucking house and cannery on the Washington coast, now listed on the National Register of Historic Places. The farm's co-owner, Dan Driscoll, became active in the industry at age six, stringing oyster shells to make cultch for his uncle Dick Sheldon, owner of the still-extant Northern Oyster Company. Now Dan and Katherine Driscoll, his business partner and wife, harvest their farm-reared

Pacific oysters by hand, scrubbing their shells to remove the encrusting algae, sorting them, and stuffing them in sacks to be shipped to restaurants and distributors throughout the Northwest, as well as Chicago, Miami, and Washington DC. "Our mission is to keep the Oyster in Oysterville," says Katherine. The Driscolls' outgoing personalities and their charming farm's picturesque location on the outskirts of town are helpful tools toward achieving this goal.

The Driscolls aren't alone in their efforts to preserve the culture that has evolved around oyster-growing. Not only oyster growers, but bank officers, natural resource managers, curators of regional history museums, hoteliers—all have played active parts in keeping this unique industry alive. Because of their efforts, the Pacific Northwest is now filled with highly visible signs of the industry's role in shaping the resource-dependent communities of its scenic coasts. Among the many icons of the oyster's importance are roadside placards, enticing travelers to pull over and purchase fresh-picked products of nearby beds; posters and T-shirts for events like the Oyster Stampede Festival, hosted each spring in the streets of South Bend, Washington, or the West Coast Oyster Shucking Competition, a tourney for professional oyster openers, held annually in Shelton, Washington; and, of course, Dan and Louis' Oyster Bar in Portland, Oregon, or any of the many restaurants featuring the pride of the Pacific—sautéed, steamed, barbecued, or served raw on the half shell, with a squeeze of lemon.

"When the tide is out, the table is set," one beachcomber's adage maintains. Nowhere is that table more attractively displayed than on the tide-swept beaches of the Pacific Northwest, whose beds are a heaven on the half shell, occupied by the bivalve the world loves best.

OH MY, PIE

If stew is not your brew but you want something equally warm and hearty, what could be better than a rich and homey pot pie? Oysters bake well, and when topped with crusty, buttery biscuit, well, what more can we say? Oyster pie is a traditional New Orleans dish, but for this recipe, author and columnist Jay Harlow of the San Francisco *Examiner* added the buttery taste of artichoke. Since the pie is not that colorful, he also recommends using a colored baking dish, or serving it with other foods that will bring color to the presentation.

OYSTER AND ARTICHOKE POT PIES

4 medium or large artichokes (about 2 pounds)
1²/₃ cups all-purpose flour
2¹/₂ tsp. baking powder
³/₄ tsp. salt
Scant cup whipping cream
2 jars (10 oz. each) small oysters, drained, liquor reserved
3 T. butter
1 finely diced yellow onion
¹/₂ cup finely diced green onion
¹/₄ tsp. Creole seafood seasoning
3 T. flour
¹/₄ cup water or milk (approximately)
Salt and pepper to taste

Steam or boil artichokes until just done (about 45 minutes). Let cool. Remove outer leaves, keeping bases intact. Discard smallest inner leaves and chokes. Dice bottoms. (Optional: scrape pulp from insides of leaves and set aside, or reserve leaves to serve as separate course.) Biscuit topping: combine all-purpose flour, baking powder and salt in large mixing bowl and mix thoroughly. Stir in cream with a fork, just until mixture is evenly moistened. Turn mixture by hand into a bowl until most of the floury bits are absorbed. Cover dough and let it rest at least 15 minutes.

Drain oysters thoroughly, retaining liquid. Melt butter in a saucepan over medium heat. Remove 1 tablespoon and set aside. Add both types of onion and seasoning and cook until soft. Stir in flour and cook, stirring until lightly browned. Add water or milk to the oyster liquor if needed to make 1 cup. Stir into saucepan with scraped artichoke pulp and cook until quite thick. Taste and adjust for seasoning; set aside to cool. Preheat oven to 350°F. Divide oysters and diced artichoke bottoms among four ovenproof individual casseroles (large oysters may be cut into bite-size pieces). Spoon sauce over all. Turn biscuit dough onto lightly floured board and press with hands to ¹/₈" to ¹/₄" thick. Cut dough into quarters and thin more as needed to fit casseroles. Top each casserole with dough, sealing dough against edges and trimming excess. Brush tops with melted butter. Cut three or four small vents in the top of each pie. Bake until crusts are golden brown, about 30 minutes. Makes four servings.

(From: *West Coast Seafood* by Jay Harlow. Sasquatch Books, Seattle, 1999)

Oyster and Artichoke Pot Pies (opposite). This vintage display card for Hood Canal–grown oysters (opposite, below) comes from the collection of Dick Steele.

EATING AT XINH'S

Once you've seen Chef Xinh Dwelley at work in her kitchen, you may wonder why you bother cooking at home. One of the fastest shuckers in the west, Xinh won the West Coast oyster shucking championship several years in a row. Her long-time employers at Taylor Seafood knew she was a gem, but when she started cooking their shellfish products they realized she was in the wrong setting. Her meals were so impressive, they helped get her started in her own restaurant business in Shelton, where she delights customers with creative concoctions of oysters, clams, and mussels. The title of this recipe alone is enough to transport your tastebuds.

OYSTER SAUTÉ IN ASIAN SAUCE

1 quart fresh shucked oysters, any size
2 T. butter or vegetable oil
1 T. minced garlic
¹/₂ chopped onion
1 tsp. lemon grass
1 T. Hoisin sauce
1 T. oyster sauce
1 T. cooking sherry
Juice of ¹/₂ fresh lemon
2 stalks thinly sliced celery
1 cup sliced red & green peppers
1 T. sesame seed oil
1 T. soy sauce (optional)
3 chopped green onions
1 T. chopped fresh cilantro (optional)
Black pepper to taste

In a large saucepan, boil one quart of salted water. Add the oysters, and stir gently for 2–3 minutes. Remove the oysters from the pan, wash and rinse, set aside. In a large sauté pan, heat oil or butter, add garlic, onion, and lemon grass and sauté approximately 1 minute. Add oysters and simmer 2–3 minutes. Add remaining ingredients. Simmer, stirring gently until heated through. Add cilantro and green onions, and stir well. Serve over steamed rice.

(From: Xinh Dwelley, Chef, Xinh's Clam and Oyster House, Shelton, Washington, 2000)

TASTE, AND THEN SOME

Shellfish culture is now the number one employer on Cortes Island, British Columbia, and one of the largest employers in the Baynes Sound area. Here, aquaculture is a source of local pride, exemplified by the British Columbia Shellfish Growers Association which describes the local oyster as having a "fresh and crisp taste [that] imparts a feeling of both opulence and adventure!" Considering that, no ordinary oyster will do!

The following recipe comes from Fanny Bay, a small community on the East Coast of Vancouver Island, where oyster exporters nurture the Fanny Bay oyster to distinction.

OYSTER PEPPER POT

4 chopped onions
2 cloves garlic
4 cups chopped celery
2 cups chopped mushrooms
2 pints Heinz Home Style Chile sauce
1 28 oz. can tomatoes
4 diced peppers
Flour
1 quart fresh, shucked oysters, chopped
Salt & pepper to taste,
Basil & oregano to taste

Simmer first 6 ingredients together 1 to 2 hours. In the last half hour of cooking, add peppers. Thicken with flour if necessary. Add the raw, chopped oysters and their juice to the pot 5 minutes before serving. Season to taste.

(From: Fanny Bay Oysters Ltd., Union Bay, British Columbia, Canada, acquired from Linda Purvis at the Courtenay Fish and Game Club, 2000)

Then and now: the Whistling Oyster in Quilcene has attracted oyster aficionados for nearly eight decades.

NOTES

CHAPTER I
AN OYSTERMAN'S LOT (PP 11–25)

Few natural history texts are as fancifully written as *Oysters Have Eyes* or *The Travels of a Pacific Oyster* by Eldon Griffith (Seattle: Wilberlilla Publishers, 1941). "Who has not exchanged the trusting handshake of friendship with the prank-playing person who holds [an oyster] concealed in his palm?" the book asks, and we are hard pressed to answer.

The inherent health benefits of oysters and other shellfish are neatly presented by University of Washington professor Faye M. Dong in *The Nutritional Value of Shellfish*, a Washington Sea Grant publication. M. F. K. Fisher's *Consider the Oyster* (New York: North Pointe Press, 1954) is another good source of nutritional data—and recipes—for our beloved bivalve. The recipe circa 1390 appears in *On Food and Cooking* by Harold McGee (New York: Scribners, 1984), a must-have for any serious seafood gourmand.

Information about British oyster culture comes from *Oysters* by C. M. Younge (London: Collins, 1960), the authority on all things malacological. The dawn of Pacific oyster farming is described in *Japanese Oyster-Culture*, a bulletin of the U.S. Fish Commission (volume 22, 1902) by Bashford Dean, then adjunct professor of Zoology at Columbia University.

CHAPTER 2
BEFORE THE FIRST FARMS (PP 27–49)

This chapter's epigraph is from *The Oyster Was Our World: Life on Oyster Bay, 1898 to 1914* (Seattle: Shorey Book Store, 1976), a charming depiction of the golden days of oyster farming in Puget Sound. "Those days of oystering come back with overtones of excitement and happiness. We sang as we culled. Pearl and I recited poems and Pap gave us the gist of works of Jules Verne, Tom Paine, Mark Twain, and Edward Bellamy."

Since modern photographic techniques had yet to be perfected, scenes of San Francisco's earliest oyster enterprises are best visualized as lithographs and hand-me-down tales of the fellows who worked the flats. More difficult to imagine was the shellfish mania that swept the nation back then. "In Illinois about the time of the gold rush, an ambitious former congressman named Abraham Lincoln entertained his friends and associates at buffets at which oysters—and nothing but oysters—were prepared in every conceivable way," wrote Joseph R. Conlin in *Bacon, Beans and Galantines: Food and Foodways on the Western Mining Frontier* (Reno: University of Nevada Press, 1986). "Take two hundred fat oysters" one recipe by Eliza Leslie, the Julia Child of the mid-1800s, begins.

Although he failed to write what he was paid for—a report on the cultures of Northwest coastal Natives—correspondent James Swan compiled an equally compelling tale in "Three Years at Shoal-Water Bay," one of several exciting sections of his classic *The Northwest Coast* (Seattle: University of Washington Press, 1998).

Emerson J. Watson's memoirs appear in Volume VIII, Numbers 3 and 4 (1973) of *The Sou'Wester*, the quarterly journal of the Pacific County, Washington, Historical Society.

CHAPTER 3
COLLECTORS BECOME CULTIVATORS (PP 51–81)

Definitive data on the early days of Northwest oystering is difficult to obtain. However, three authoritative overviews exist: "The Shellfish Industry of California—Past, Present, and Future" by William N. Shaw (in NOAA Technical Report NMFS 128, U.S. Department of Commerce, 1997); "Report of Observations Respecting the Oyster Resources and Oyster Fishery of the Pacific Coast of the United States," by Charles H. Townsend (in *Report of the Commissioner of Fish and Fisheries*, 1893); and *The California Oyster Industry* by E. M. Barrett (Fish Bulletin 123, California Department of Fish and Game, 1963).

A less than objective assessment of the eastern oyster industry in Willapa Bay is contained in a special supplement to the *Willapa Harbor Pilot* of 1900, reprinted by the *South Bend Journal* newspaper. "Unlike the American pig, the American oyster goes unchallenged through the markets of the nations," the supplement states. "His primacy among the bivalves of the world is indisputable. Of the various oysters which uncover for the Stars and Stripes, none surpass and few can equal the Epicurean flavor of the native product of Willapa Bay."

The details of the eastern oyster's introduction are presented by R. W. Doane in "A Preliminary Report Reflecting the Investigations Relative to the Propagation of the Eastern Oyster in the State of Washington" (in *First Report of the State Fish Commission*, 1901). Humphrey Nelson's adventures in oysterdom are described in *The Little Man and the Little Oyster* (Belfair, Washington: Mason County Historical Society, 1990).

For his theory about the economic doom of eastern oysters and a crash course on the evolution of Northwest oyster boats, we are grateful to Bruce Weilepp, director of the Pacific County Historical Museum.

CHAPTER 4
THE PACIFIC OYSTER PREMIERES (PP 83-103)

The best biography of the Pacific oyster in Washington is E. N. Steele's *The Immigrant Oyster* (Ostrea gigas) *Now Known as the Pacific Oyster* (Olympia: Warren's Quick Print, 1964), the sequel to his *Rise and Decline of the Olympia Oyster* (Elma, Washington: Fulco Publications, 1957). Other solid sources include Trevor Kincaid's self-published *The Ecology of Willapa Bay, Washington, in Relation to the Oyster Industry* (Seattle: 1968) and his more populist *Oyster Industry of Willapa Bay, Washington* (Seattle: Caliostoma Company, 1951). Ample biographical information on Kincaid is best condensed by Deborah L. Illman in *Pathbreakers: A Century of Excellence in Science and Technology at the University of Washington* (Seattle: University of Washington Office of Research, 1996).

Following in Kincaid's footsteps, Nancy Lloyd researched, wrote, and illustrated the highly readable *Willapa Bay & The Oysters* (Oysterville: Oysterville Hand Print, 1999), whose text explains why Willapa oysters are so "dependably wholesome." Lloyd was instrumental in creating the interpretive center at Nahcotta, Washington—an important destination for any student of regional history or collector of oyster-abilia.

CHAPTER 5
OYSTERS IN WAR AND PEACE (PP 105-125)

The plight of Japanese-American oyster growers during World War II was depicted in two sources—*Longlines*, the bi-monthly newsletter of the Pacific Coast Oyster Growers Association and the *Chinook Observer*, which published an interview with Richard Murakami on February 25, 1992—and of course, extensive conversations with the growers themselves.

From Al Qualmann's *Blood on the Half Shell* (Portland: Binford & Mort, 1983), we gathered details on Willapa Bay's postwar years. The inside scoop on Japanese oyster drills came from another knowledgeable Northwesterner, Clyde Sayce, whose treatise "The Oyster Industry of Willapa Bay" appeared in *Proceedings of the Symposium on Terrestrial and Aquatic Ecological Studies of the Northwest* (Eastern Washington State College Press, Cheney, Washington, 1976).

From a *Longlines* interview with Dick Steele and a conversation with Cedric Lindsay, we learned how the Dabob Bay seed industry was born. The book's discussion of seed sources in British Columbia's Pendrill Sound is based on material from *Pacific Oyster Culture in British Columbia* by D. B. Quayle (Ottawa: Canadian Bulletin of Fisheries and Aquatic Sciences 218, 1988).

Ed Gruble helped us piece together an informal history of oyster stew, while biologist Chuck Woelke gave us the inside story on the Kumamoto oyster's introduction.

CHAPTER 6
FROM BOOM TO BUST AND BACK (PP 127-155)

The epigraph for this chapter is from an interview with Jim Kemmer, a second-generation oyster grower, commercial fisher, and timber worker from Ilwaco, Washington. "Hard work, but it's worth it," Jim says about oystering. "And I'm my own boss—that's important." Patrick Tomberlin, a sixth grader at Ilwaco's Hilltop School, conducted the interview.

The oystermen's battles with polluters have been well documented, most recently in a *Seattle Post-Intelligencer* article, published in February 2000. Although Steele and Nelson's books contain plenty of first-hand information, the best overview of this struggle is in Daniel Chasan's *The Water Link: A History of Puget Sound as a Resource* (Seattle: Washington Sea Grant Program, 1981).

The conflict with foreign competitors is not nearly as well documented. For insights into this thorny issue, we're indebted to oysterman Lee Wiegardt and to Cedric Lindsay's "The Fisheries for Olympia Oysters, *Ostreola conchaphila*; Pacific Oysters, *Crassostrea gigas*; and Pacific Razor Clams, *Silqua patula*, in the State of Washington," (NOAA Technical Report NMFS 128, , U.S. Department of Commerce, 1997).

Lindsay's NOAA report was also helpful for its data on oyster hatcheries. Combined with Lee Hansen's essay "Remote Setting: a Brief History" (published in *Remote Setting and Nursery Culture for Shellfish Growers*, a 1991 workshop record by Washington Sea Grant Program), and further insights from Point Whitney lab's Hal Beattie, Taylor Shellfish's hatchery manager Ed Jones, and shellfish biologists Chuck Woelke and Kenneth Chew, an authoritative history of this enterprise emerged.

Easily the most accessible information on the status of the West Coast's harmful algal blooms is contained in *Red Tides*, a newsletter published by the Northwest Fisheries Science Center and Washington Sea Grant Program in Seattle.

ACKNOWLEDGMENTS

Like a farmed oyster, this book could not exist without a nurturing environment and some special care. We are especially grateful to the many individuals who so graciously supported our work. For their generous financial support as patrons to this project, we thank the owners of Pierre Ford, Coast Seafood, Little Skookum Shellfish Growers, Taylor Shellfish Company, Rock Point Oyster Company, and Wiegardt Brothers, Inc. For their support as associates to this project, we thank the owners of Blau Oyster Company, Minterbrook Oyster Company, Norplex, Inc., and Western Oyster Company. For additional financial support we also thank Baywater, Inc., B J Seafood Farm, Dahman Shellfish Company, Nisbet Oyster Company, Northern Oyster Company, and Olympia Oyster Company.

For assistance in shaping the manuscript, we thank University of Washington professors David Armstrong, Kenneth Chew, and Faye Dong, UW Fisheries-Oceanography librarian Pamela Mofjeld, UW Manuscripts, Special Collections and University Archives head Carla Rickerson, historians Doug Allen, Nancy Lloyd, and Bruce Weilepp, and shellfish biologists and oystermen Bill Dewey, Ed Gruble, Rick Harbo, Cedric Lindsay, Wayne Morris, Richard Murakami, Clyde Sayce, Dick Sheldon, Dick Steele, Justin Taylor, Lee Wiegardt, Mark Wiegardt, Chuck Woelke, and Jerry Yamashita. For bringing the text to life on the book's pages, we thank senior graphic designer Robin Ricks of Washington Sea Grant Program. For their support during project development and execution, we thank Louie Echols, Andrea Copping, and Alan Krekel of Washington Sea Grant Program. For their roles in project production we gratefully acknowledge Miriam Bulmer, Robin Downey of the Pacific Coast Shellfish Growers Association, La Neu of the University of Washington, and Cynthia Nims, as well as Susan E. Cook, Kathi Cowden, Nina Hadley, Susan Hester, and Sue Raub of Washington Sea Grant Program. Special thanks to Rachel Bard for literary advice and to Doug Pfeiffer, Tim Frew, Mary Ransome, Tricia Brown, Ellen Wheat, and Kathy Matthews of Graphic Arts Center Publishing Company.

Photo Credits

Bancroft Library, University of California, Berkeley, pp. 27, 29; Beebe, Morton/Corbis, 46; Braasch, Gary/Corbis, 50; California State Archives, Sacramento, 48; Corbis, 37; Davis, Joth, 137; de Selve, Leonard/Corbis, 55; Dewey, Bill/Taylor Shellfish, 105, 109; Dumbauld, Brett, 142; Franken, Owen/Corbis, 129; Freeman, Michael/Corbis, 18 (lower right); Gordon, David G./Washington Sea Grant Program, 116; Gruble, Ed, 117, 124, 127; Harrold, Craig, cover (center), 31, 83, 85, 119, 140, 148; Holmes, Robert/ Corbis, 18 (upper left); Hopley, Mary L., 51; Ilwaco Heritage Museum, 67, 32 (Charles Doupe Collection), 99 (Fitzpatrick Collection); Jefferson County Historical Society, 35, 155 (lower left); Jensen, Greg, 139; Krantz, Ray/ Corbis, 76; Levin, Joel, 57, 78, 100 (left), 122, 152 (left); Mathers, Michael, front cover (center right), 1, 10, 27, 77, 80, 82, 104, 126, 144, 159; McNamara, Rory C., 149; Muench, David/Corbis, 2; MSCUA, University of Washington Libraries, 41, 45; MSCUA, University of Washington Libraries, Kincaid Collection, 3, 25, 33 (upper right), 40, 43, 62, 70, 71, 75, 86, 89, 91, 93, 111, 112, 114, 120, 131; Murakami Family, 106; National Marine Fisheries Service, 145; O'Rear, Charles/ Corbis, cover (lower left); Oregon Historical Society, cover, upper left (#Gi7203), 33 left (#Gi7201), 53 (#Gi7203), 63 (#Gi7202) , 73 upper right (#Gi7200); Pacific County Historical Society, 69 (PCHS# 1998.63.44), 72 (Isabel Trezise, donor), 73 lower right (PCHS#1994.71.1), 74 right (PCHS#1998.63.52), 97 (PCHS#1998.63.47); Susan Parish Collection, 65 (Joe Jeffers), 95, 110, 141 (Vibert Jeffers); Pierre Family, 7; Ricks, Robyn/ Washington Sea Grant Program, back cover; Rogers, Joel W., 59, 128; Rogers, Joel W./Corbis, 13; Schofield, Phil, 11, 15, 20, 60, 132, 133, 150, 151; Seaborn, Charles, 58; Small, Richard, Washington Sea Grant Program, 74 (right); Sneddon, James O., University of Washington, Seattle, 135; Stenjem, Scott, 4, 5, 88, 107, 146, 155 (lower left); Thompson, J.W., 147; Washington State Historical Society, 39 (Curtis #19971); Wiegardt, Lee, 16; Wiegardt, Mark, 96; Yamashita, Michael S./Corbis, 21.

Food styling by Lisa Irwin and Kitty Harmon.

INDEX